MW01480839

The Irish Terrier

– A Complete Anthology of the Dog –

1860-1940

© Vintage Dog Books 2010
This book is copyright and may not be
reproduced or copied in any way without
the express permission of the publisher in writing

ISBN No.
978-14455-2622-5 (Paperback)
978-14455-2742-0 (Hardback)

British Library Cataloguing-in-Publication Data
A catalogue record for this book is available from
the British Library

VDB

www.vintagedogbooks.com

Contents

Containing chapters from the following sources:

THE IRISH TERRIER.

By GEORGE R. KREHL.

I believe I am only repeating an admitted fact when I say that the progress of this breed in the last few years is almost without precedent. In 1878 the original supporters and discoverers of the breed were dropping off for want of encouragement. Amongst these I would name Messrs. Ridgway, Pim, Jameson, Erwin, and Crosbie Smith. The Messrs. Carey still owned a good kennel, and Mr. Wm. Graham bred them more for work than show. Mr. E. F. Despard was winning with his Sporter (now in the possession of the writer), and his sons Tanner and Tanner II. The mother of these pups, Belle, was a very large grey bitch of the old sort. The old dog Sport was still being exhibited, and Banshee, a big bitch with a generous amount of bull in her, was a *champion*. The show bench at this period presented anything but a level appearance. At the time my brother and I

1

MR. G. JAMISON'S IRISH TERRIER "SPUDS."

entered the ranks of the Irish terriers' admirers, I believe there were not more than two English exhibitors besides ourselves. The many ridiculous awards of inexperienced judges exasperated the exhibitors, and at my suggestion the Irish Terrier Club was started. It is impossible to deny the·influence exerted by the foundation of the club upon the improvement of the breed. In Ireland it awakened the interest that lay dormant; in England it served to reveal to fanciers the existence of a game and little known terrier. It is now one of the most powerful subsidiary clubs. An Irish nobleman, Viscount Castlerosse, is its president, there are Irish and English vice-presidents, two hon. secs., a treasurer, and a mixed committee of ten, and about eighty members. It has issued a code of points and a list of gentlemen qualified to act as judges.

The rise of the breed is most marked by the fact that in the days referred to one class was barely filled at the Kennel Club shows. At the last Alexandra Palace Show I had five classes to judge, with an entry of thirty-three. Besides the London shows, it was only in Ireland that classes were given for Irish terriers; now no show, English or Scotch, of any consequence issues a schedule without one or two for this breed. The appearance of Mr. Ridgway's paper in "Dogs of the British Islands" also gave a considerable fillip to the breed; and even now there is little to add to the information therein contained. Mr. Ridgway, in favour of the purity of the breed, tells us with authority that they are indigenous to their native country, and mentions that fanciers can remember them fifty and sixty years ago. He also bears testimony to their being "particularly hardy, and able to bear any amount of wet, cold, and hardship without showing the slightest symptoms of fatigue. Their coat also being a hard and wiry one, they can hunt the thickest gorse or furze covert without the slightest inconvenience." Modern fanciers are able to indorse the correctness of every word in this description of their working qualities, and his further evidence of their "usefulness, intelligence, and gameness." Mr. Ridgway also writes: "As to their capability for taking the water, and hunting in it, as well as on land, I may mention as one instance that a gentleman in the adjoining county of Tipperary has kept a pack of these terriers for years, with which he will hunt an otter as well as any pack of pure otterhounds can."

Mr. Ridgway's perfect knowledge of the breed is shown in his code of points. All the discussions in the newspapers that I have taken part in have been, not for the airing of any particular crotchets of my own, but for the maintenance and upholding in their integrity to the letter of the Ridgway points, as against the endeavours of others to convince the public that the Irish terrier is a red fox terrier. The Irish Terrier Club's points are Mr. Ridgway's elaborated and explained. Importance is placed on the shape and general appearance of the dog, which should be easy and graceful; the lines of the body should be *speedy*, without signs of heaviness or anything approaching the cobby and cloddy. Mr. T. Erwin truly said of them that, though game as fighting cocks, they should look more like running than fighting. A sufficient amount of substance is quite compatible with this structure. There is an extensive medium between the "bone" of the

3

whippit and that of a carthorse. It would not give a stranger a bad impression to describe them as a miniature Irish wolfhound in appearance. If I were asked to name the most prominent characteristics in the temperament of the Irish terrier, I should reply, " Courage and good temper."

Their courage is quite national in its quality, being of that dashing, reckless, "dare-devil" description that is associated with the human habitants of their native country. The Irish Terrier fears nothing that ever came on four legs with a furry skin. They have no caution in their gameness, but go straight at their enemy with a heedless pluck utterly regardless of consequences. They do not always conquer, but they do or die unless pulled off. It would occupy too much space to relate a few of the many instances of their courage publicly recorded.

I have read in the newspapers of a nine weeks' old pup killing a rat; of another puppy freshly cropped, with unhealed ears, rushing by older dogs of a different breed, and fiercely attacking and killing a fox, undergoing the whole time without a whimper the most terrible punishment. I know several that have killed their badger; and a letter in my possession describes an Homeric combat under water between an Irish terrier and an otter—the latter eventually succumbing. Their other quality is quite as bright a side to their character. Their good temper is remarkable in so game a terrier. Terrier men will bear me out that a quarrelsome dog is seldom truly game. I question whether any of my colleagues in the Irish Terrier Club can give an instance of one of the breed biting a human being. They are, therefore, peculiarly fitted for house-dogs where there are women and children. They make the most admirable companions, faithful, intelligent, and always full of high spirits. Whether accompanying their master out walking, following a trap or a bicycle, their never tiring liveliness will amuse their master and relieve his loneliness. The poaching blood they inherit from their ancestors gives them an instinctive love of a gun. Sportsmen have not failed to recognise their advantages as rabbiting dogs. They hunt mute. They are a peculiarly hardy breed and seldom succumb to the many ills that puppyhood is heir to. Shows have done much for their outward appearance, and without that softening effect on the temperament which usually follows in its wake. It would be a poor show where perfection could not be made up with different parts from the body of the exhibits. " Spuds," the subject of the illustration, was a beautiful bitch in her youth and when in proper coat, she shows the long, parallel, wolfhound-like head. Her coat was as hard as cocoa-nut fibre, the colour, a bright yellow red, the hue of September wheat, with the sun on it. She is properly leggy, long rather in body, and yet firmly knit together, and very full of the racing-build. The golden wheaten is also a good colour, but the mahogany red one sometimes sees is to be avoided as showing the bar sinister of the black and tan. Long legs and a smooth face are necessary characteristics; and short legs, profuse coat, and long hair on the face indicate mongrelism and Scotch blending. Much of the breed's recent advance is due to the improved knowledge of the judges. While such pitiful blunders in the awards were an every show occurrence, it was rather a wonder the breed did not deteriorate instead of only standing still. To-day I may safely say they rival in

4

popularity the oldest established breeds, and to the man who values qualities above looks, I would repeat that for a good-tempered and game dog, a rough-and-ready tyke that will fight anything and fear nothing there is no better than the Irish Terrier.

IRISH TERRIER CLUB'S CODE OF POINTS.

Positive Points.	Value.	Negative Points.	Value.
Head, jaw, teeth and eyes	15	White nails, toes and feet ...... *minus* 10	
Ears	5	Much white on chest	10
Legs and feet	10	Ears cropped	5
Neck	5	Mouth undershot or cankered	10
Shoulders and chest	10	Coat shaggy, curly, or soft	10
Back and loin	10	Uneven in colour	5
Hind quarters and stern	10		
Coat	15		
Colour	10		
Size and symmetry	10		
Total	**100**	**Total**	**50**

Disqualifying Points :—Nose, cherry or red. Brindle colour.

DESCRIPTIVE PARTICULARS.

Head.—Long ; skull flat, and rather narrow between ears, getting slightly narrower towards the eye ; free from wrinkle; stop hardly visible, except in profile. The jaw must be strong and muscular, but not too full in the cheek, and of a good punishing length, but not so fine as a white English terrier's. There should be a slight falling away below the eye, so as not to have a greyhound appearance. Hair on face of same description as on body, but short (about a quarter of an inch long), in appearance almost smooth and straight; a slight beard is the only longish hair (and is only long in comparison with the rest) that is permissible, and that is characteristic.

Teeth.—Should be strong and level.

Lips.—Not so tight as a bull-terrier's but well-fitting, showing through the hair their black lining.

Nose.—Must be black.

Ears.—When uncut, small and V-shaped, of moderate thickness, set well up on the head, and dropping forward closely to the cheek. The ears must be free of fringe, and the hair thereon shorter and generally darker in colour than the body.

Neck.—Should be of a fair length, and gradually widening towards the shoulders, well carried, and free of throatiness. There is generally a slight sort of frill visible at each side of the neck, running nearly to the corner of the ear, which is looked on as very characteristic.

Shoulders and chest.—Shoulders must be fine, long, and sloping well into the back; the chest deep and muscular, but neither full nor wide.

Back and loin.—Body moderately long; back should be strong and straight, with no appearance of slackness behind the shoulders; the loin broad and powerful

5

and slightly arched; ribs fairly sprung, rather deep than round, and well ribbed back.

Hind quarters.—Well under the dog should be strong and muscular, the thighs powerful, hocks near the ground, stifles not much bent.

Stern.—Generally docked, should be free of fringe or feather, set on pretty high, carried gaily, but not over the back or curled.

Feet and legs.—Feet should be strong, tolerably round, and moderately small; toes arched, and neither turned out nor in; black toe-nails are preferable and most desirable. Legs moderately long, well set from the shoulders, perfectly straight, with plenty of bone and muscle; the elbows working freely clear of the sides, pasterns short and straight, hardly noticeable. Both fore and hind legs should be moved straight forward when travelling, the stifles not turned outwards, the legs free of feather and covered like the head, with as hard a texture of coat as body, but not so long.

Coat.—Hard and wiry, free of softness or silkiness, not so long as to hide the outlines of the body, particularly in the hindquarters, straight and flat, no shagginess, and free of lock or curl.

Colour.—Should be "whole coloured," the most desirable being bright red; next wheaten, yellow, and grey, brindle disqualifying. White sometimes appears on chest and feet; it is more objectionable on the latter than on the chest, as a speck of white on chest is frequently to be seen in all self-coloured breeds.

Size and symmetry.—Weight in show condition, from 16lb. to 24lb.—say 16lb. to 22lb. for bitches and 18lb. to 24lb. for dogs. The most desirable weight is 22lb. or under, which is a nice stylish and useful size. The dog must present an active, lively, lithe, and wiry appearance; lots of substance, at the same time free of clumsiness, as speed and endurance, as well as power, are very essential. They must be neither "cloddy" nor "cobby," but should be framed on the "lines of speed," showing a graceful "racing outline."

The subject of the illustration is Spuds (K.C.S.B. 6846), bred by Mr. George Jamison, Newtownards, Ireland. Spuds has won the following prizes: Cork, 2nd prize, 1876, Mr. Ridgway, judge; Newtownards, 1st prize and special cup for best in four Irish terrier classes, Mr. Skidmore, judge; Brighton, 2nd prize, Mr. Sam Handley, judge; Lisburn, 1877, 1st prize, Mr. Skidmore, judge; Newtownards, 1877, 1st prize and special cup for best in two Irish terrier classes, Mr. J. J. Pim, judge; Agricultural Hall, London, 2nd prize, Colonel Cowen, judge; Bristol, 1st prize, Mr. Percival, judge; Alexandra Palace, 1st prize, Mr. Handley, judge.

6

THE IRISH TERRIER.

As a breed these dogs are peculiarly adapted to the country, being particularly hardy and able to bear any amount of wet, cold and hardship without showing the slightest symptoms of fatigue. Their coat, also, being a hard and wiry one, they can hunt the thickest gorse or furze covert without the slightest inconvenience.

For usefulness, intelligence and gameness, as well as general appearance, are second to no other breed of terrier.

POINTS AND PROPERTIES.

Head.—Long and rather narrow across skull, flat, and perfectly free from stop or wrinkle.

Muzzle.—Long and rather pointed, but strong in make, with good black nose, and free from loose flesh and chop.

Teeth.—Perfectly level, and evenly set in good strong jaws.

Ears.—When uncut, small and filbert-shaped, and lying close to head; color sometimes darker than rest of body; hair on ears short and free from fringe.

Neck.—Tolerably long and well arched.

Legs.—Moderately long, well set from the shoulders, with plenty of bone and muscle; must be perfectly straight, and covered, like the ears and head, with a similar texture of coat as the body, but not quite so long.

Eyes.—Small, keen and hazel color.

Feet.—Strong, tolerably round, with toes well split up; most pure specimens have black toe-nails.

Chest.—Muscular and rather deep, but should not be either full or wide.

Body.—Moderately long, with ribs well sprung; loin and back should show great strength, and all well knit together.

Coat.—Must be hard, rough and wiry, in decided contradistinction to softness, shagginesss and silkiness, and all parts perfectly free from lock or curl. Hair on head and legs is not quite so long as rest of body.

Color most desired is red, and the brighter the color the better; next in order, wheaten or yellow, and gray; but brindle is to be objected to, thereby showing intermixture of the bull breed.

Tail, if uncut, carried gaily, without a ring, and showing absence of feather and bushiness.

Weight of good working Irish terriers varies from 17lb. to 25lb.

THE Irish Terrier is a marvellous instance of the improvement which the steady and combined perseverance of breeders can bring about in a variety of dog in the space of a few years. A decade ago the breed was practically unknown, and now the Irish Terrier class is one of the interesting features of our greatest shows. Like other breeds, it had to be known to be appreciated at its proper value; and like other breeds, when it once gained a fair footing amongst "doggy" men, supporters sprung up on all sides. With the Irish Terrier it is essentially the fact that "handsome is as handsome does," for though valuing the breed for the position it has gained as a vermin dog, we are fain to admit that in personal attractions it is not equal to many other varieties. A good, game, hard dog, his workmanlike jacket and somewhat plain outline are in themselves likely to escape the observation of any but an ardent dog-lover; but there is a spirit within the dog which, when discovered, must make him friends wherever he goes. The improvement to which allusion has been already made is mainly due to the energy and perseverance of a very few gentlemen; and as most of the future prize dogs of this breed may reasonably be expected to spring from the best-known winners which have been recently exhibited, we propose, before going into the characteristics and description of the breed, to give a brief summary of the best dogs up to the present time, and the several positions they have occupied in the leading prize-lists.

At Belfast in June, 1875, an Irish Terrier Club was for the first time spoken of, but nothing came of it. Before this time a discussion upon the points of the breed had been going on in the *Live Stock Journal*, and in July, 1875, an illustration was given of two of Dr. Mark's dogs. The illustration, however, does not represent the modern type of Irish Terriers at all; they look like Scotch Terriers with a few drops of Irish blood in them. They have long hair all over the head and neck, and it actually parts down the centre; what could be more Scotch? The picture is worth preserving as showing what the head of an Irish Terrier should not be. A correspondent, writing at the time, described this picture in the following words:—"The very look of them is enough to convince any fair-thinking man that Scotch blood is in their composition. We will take, for instance, the dog at the left-hand side, which I find is the splendid game bitch Kate. Look at the head and face of this dog; if Scotch blood is not stamped on it then I know nothing. Look at the long hair on the forehead, with the vein or equal division in the centre. Look again at the long hair on the muzzle and under the jaw, and if, as I say, this does not denote the Scotch cross, and a good deal of it, then I know nothing about the points which constitute an Irish Terrier. The surest sign of Scotch blood in a rough Terrier is the length of hair on forehead. Another thing which goes to prove the Scotch cross is the vein or furrow running up the centre of the forehead. This is not to be met with in Irish Terriers."

At Belfast, in July, 1875, appeared the best lot of Irish Terriers brought together up to that date. Mr. D. O'Connell was represented with Slasher, a capital stamp of a hard, wiry-

coated, working Terrier, said to be a pure old white Irish Terrier, a splendid field and water dog. Newtownards, September, 1875, saw Mr. Morton's Fly to the fore, with Sport (under his new name, Celt) second. In the *Live Stock Journal*, August 20th, 1875, had already appeared an engraving, which is reproduced in this work, of Sport, then the property of Mr. George Jamison. This portrait was hailed with delight on all sides as representing the genuine true-bred Irish Terrier; and so it does. It may be remarked that this dog was shown often, only again and again to be beaten by curs that had no right to be

DR. MARK'S KATE AND BADGER.

in the same show with him ; in fact, wherever Sport was shown in a dog class, until 1878, when Sporter appeared in the field, there was no dog he should have been put second to; and Mr. Jamison must be congratulated on his pluck in sticking so well to his colours in spite of constant disappointments. At Lisburn, in 1876; Sport was second to the late Banshee (who died a champion after a singularly lucky and successful show career, and also the property of Mr. George Jamison at that time). Banshee was then only a youngster of thirteen months, and not only gained the first prize but cup as well.

At Dublin, in March, 1876, took place the show over which such a commotion was afterwards raised. The variety was more than charming, it was ridiculous ; reports say there was no attempt at type in particular, no style; long legs, short legs, hard coats, soft coats, thick short skulls, and long lean ones ; all were there. "Long, low, and useful dogs" were held up for admiration. Long and useful, if you like, but never *low* for an Irish

Terrier. No pride nor genuine interest was yet taken in the dog (we, of course, except one or two veteran breeders who still pluckily continued), nobody yet bothered themselves about age, breeder, or pedigree. Boxer, the first prize dog, was entered "breeder, owner, pedigree unknown." That is too deliciously Irish, his own breeder not knowing his pedigree. Another exhibitor entered his as "Shaughraun, breeder one of the famous Limerick night

MR. JAMISON'S SPORT.

watch. Pedigree too long to give, but inquisitive people can inquire at the watch-house here, and most likely they will be told." We quote this to prove the nature of many earlier pedigrees.

To come to later days, when many of the best dogs of the present time, such as Sporter, Moya Doolan, Dr. Carey's Sport, and Colleen Dhas, were well before the public, we find at Belfast, in June, 1878, Mr. Despard's Tanner (afterwards 1st Birmingham) took 1st, 2nd going to old Sport, and 3rd to W. Graham's Sporter. In bitches Kate was 1st, and Moya Doolan 2nd. In September, 1878, at Newtownards, the opinions of experts are encouraging. "It is a pleasure to look along the benches at recent shows. The eye has not the same chance it had in former years of being offended, the majority of the weeds having

12

disappeared." Mr. Graham won, with Sporter, the champion cup for the best dog or bitch exhibited. In open dogs Parnell and Tanner II. were 1st and 2nd, both since dead. In the bitches Moya Doolan beat Colleen Dhas. At Birmingham, in December, 1878, Tanner was 1st and Fly 2nd. Fly had no right to her place; and it was characteristic of the judging that Spuds was quite passed over. In December, 1878, at the Alexandra Palace, Fly (the 2nd prize winner at Birmingham) was 1st, and Spuds 2nd, Paddy II. commended, and Moya Doolan not noticed. The pent-up feelings of the Irish Terrier breeders now burst forth, and first took shape in a petition, which was to be presented to the Kennel Club, praying them in future to appoint them special judges, or, failing that, to let the same gentlemen that had wire-haired Fox-terriers also judge Irish Terriers. This latter was a good proposition, which we herewith recommend to the attention of dog-show committees; they will then get judged by a *terrier* man, and that will be a move towards satisfactory decisions. However, seeing the support which the petition promised to receive, the question was raised, Why not establish a Club at once? In a week or two the club numbered fifty, nearly half of which were Englishmen. Even so soon Irish Terrier Club was one of the greatest successes in dog clubs on record, and since that time the number and interest in it have gone on increasing. At the Irish Kennel Club Show, Dublin, in April, 1879, Spuds and Moya Doolan were 1st and 2nd in champion class; Tanner II. and Paddy II. were 1st and 2nd in open dogs; and Sting, still a puppy, made her first appearance, and won in open bitches, beating Rags and Kathleen. Gaelic was very highly commended, this being his first appearance. At the Alexandra Palace, in July, 1879, Gaelic was put over Sporter and Erin, and a new bitch over Moya Doolan.

Thus far we have endeavoured to trace the history of the Irish Terrier proper during the last few years, and now we venture to lay before our readers the experience of, and opinions on, the breed of Mr. George R. Krehl, the enthusiastic English Vice-president of the Irish Terrier Club. This gentleman, who at great personal trouble has in the kindest possible way collected for us the extracts and opinions of the most trustworthy authorities, and interwoven them with his own, writes as follows:—

"The Irish Terrier is a true and distinct breed indigenous to Ireland, and no man can trace its origin, which is lost in antiquity. Mr. Ridgway, of Waterford, whose name is familiar in Irish Terrier circles from having drawn up the first code of points, states that they have been known in Ireland 'as long as that country has been an island, and I ground my faith in their age and purity on the fact that there exist *old manuscripts in Irish* mentioning the existence of the breed at a very remote period.' In old pictures representing scenes of Irish life, an Irish Terrier or two are often to be descried. Ballymena and County Wicklow may almost claim to be the birthplaces of the breed. Most of the best specimens hail from Ballymena and the neighbourhood, where Mr. Thomas Erwin, of Irish Setter fame, boasts an extensive experience of this breed, and has always kept a few of the right old working sort for sporting purposes; and 'in County Wicklow,' Mr. Merry says, 'it is well known that the pure breed of Irish Terriers have been carefully kept distinct and highly prized for more than a century.' Mr. E. F. Despard, whose name is well known in Irish Terrier circles as a very successful breeder and exhibitor, claims an acquaintance of over 40 years with the breed. Mr. George Jamison, too, has known and kept them many years, and up till a little while ago had won more prizes than all the rest of the Breeders put together. I mention these proofs of the age of the breed to show those who have lately come to admire them that it is not a made up, composite, or mushroom breed. They are part of Ireland's national economy, and are worthily embodied in the Sportsman's toast—'Irish women, Irish horses, and Irish dogs' (which means, Irish *terriers*, setters, and spaniels).

"One's first acquaintance with this 'Pre-historic Terrier' is apt to be disappointing (except to a really 'doggy' *terrier* man), that is, because there is no meretricious flash about them; but there is that about them which you learn to like, they grow upon you. They supply the want so often expressed for 'a smart-looking dog with something in him.' There is that about their rough-and-ready appearance which can only be described as genuine terrier, or more emphatically ' *tarrier-character*.' They are *facile princeps* the sportsman's terrier, and having never yet been made fashion's darlings still retain in all its purity their instinctive love of hard work. Their characters do not suit them for ladies' pets, but render them the best dogs out for the man that loves his gun and quiet sport.

"Amongst those wise old fellows that one comes across in the country, who like a dog with something in him and a 'terrier' of course, the Irishman is prime favourite. And they know what they are about, those old fellows, and are sportsmen, too, in their own sort of way, when the sun has gone down. This reminds me of a discreditable fact in the history of Irish Terriers, that were not always only 'the poor man's sentinel,' but oftentimes something more, when by the aid of their marvellous noses and long legs they, when the shades of night had fallen, provided the pot with that which gave forth the savoury smell and imparted a flavour to the 'spuds.' This, however, if it injured their moral principles, certainly sustained their love and capability for rabbiting. In olden times, too, the larger sizes were bred and used for fighting, and there is still a dash of the old fighting blood in their descendants. They dearly love a mill, and though it would be calumny to say they are quarrelsome, yet it must be admitted that the male portion of the breed are perhaps a little too ready to resent any attempt at interfering with their coats; but are they not *Irish*, and when did an Irishman shirk a shindy? My dog Sporter is very true to character in this respect. Small dogs, or even those of his own size, he never deigns to notice; but if some large specimen of the genus *canis* approaches him, putting on 'side' and airs, Sporter immediately stiffens up visibly, his tail assumes a defiant angle above the horizontal, his ears are cocked forward alertly, and there is an ominous twitching of his upper lips which says as plain as looks can speak, 'Lave me alone, ye spalpeen.' Should his warning not be accepted, a scrimmage ensues, which I speedily terminate by whipping him up under my arm by his tail and marching him off. *En passant*, I recommend this as a very effectual and safe manner of putting a stop to a canine *mêlée*. 'Hitting off' Irish Terriers when fighting I have found useless; they think the pain comes from their opponent, and this only serves to rouse them to fresh efforts.

Now although they have always been Ireland's national terrier, yet it must be admitted, and it is only too patent, that for many years the breed had been much neglected; allowed to 'grow wild,' in fact, and left too much in the hands of one class. I cast no reflection on 'the foinest pisintry in Europe' when I say that, knowing nothing of dog-shows, they bred to no standard and kept their dogs for work; and if they thought a cross with neighbour Micky's dog would improve their own in that quality they did not stop to inquire about pedigree. In this manner the breed depreciated, and Scotch and other blood crept in to the injury of the pure breed; but, fortunately, when the tide in their favour set in the genuine breeder found plenty of pure, unadulterated material to commence upon.

"I cannot with accuracy give the date when Irish Terriers first made their advent upon the show-bench. I believe it was some time about 1870. At Dublin, in 1873, Mr. J. O'Connor's bitch Daisy won one of the first prizes given for the breed. Speaking of the breed at Newtownards Show, in 1874, where a class was given for 'Irish Rough Terriers,' the reporter says : 'We were much struck with the Irish Rough Terriers, a "varmint" looking lot of beggars, which well deserve a corner at any of our shows. They quite repaid our visit, by the way, and "widened" our experience of the genus terrier. A Dubliner present said "he'd loike to see ere a dog that 'ud bate thim." The pick was acknowledged to be Mr. Morton's " Fly," the first prize bitch. She is a compactly-built, hard-haired, yellow terrier, about 18 lbs., with a face speaking kindliness, wisdom, and pluck.' The ' Fly ' here spoken of had a very successful show career, and was the first one of the breed that earned the title 'Champion.' She was also a remarkably game bitch, and I will allude to her later when I discuss the qualities of the breed. At Dublin, in October, 1874, it is said there were a few good ones in the class. At Lisburn, in May, 1875, the dog Stinger, about which there has been so much discussion, won. It is beyond a doubt that Stinger was not of the present recognised type, he was long-backed and short-legged ; a dark blue grizzle-coloured back, tan legs, and white turned-out feet ; in fact, full of Scotch blood. His head and the texture of his coat were his only redeeming points. There were a better sort in the class than Stinger, and if, as I believe, Old Sport was there, he un-hesitatingly should have won.

" The Irish Terrier is a very intelligent dog and most lively and amusing companion. He is equally suitable for town and country. He is a mine of fun for a country ramble, putting up everything he comes across ; and there is no better terrier than a well-broken Irish for a quiet ramble round the fields with your gun. Mr. Despard aptly describes him as 'the poor man's sentinel, the farmer's friend, and generally the gentleman's favourite,' they are such merry, rough-and-ready looking fellows, and the dash of the 'devil' they all carry in their bearing makes them very attractive to terrier lovers.

" Mr. Erwin says, ' There are some strains of them that will hunt stubble, or, indeed, any kind of field or marsh, quartering their ground like a Setter or Pointer, and, more-over, standing on their game in their own style. When a lad I had a dog of this breed, over which I have shot as many as nine couple of snipe, and have been home in good time for school at ten o'clock A.M. There was little time for missing on the part of either of us, and the dog did not make a single mistake. The colour I like best is a yellowish-red.'

" Irish Terriers are not quarrelsome, but can and will take their own part if set upon, the size of the aggressor no object. Ballymena having sent more Terriers to the show-bench than any other locality that I know of, and this breed of dog having been a favourite here since I remember dogs, I have had a good opportunity of studying them, and think more highly of them the longer I know them. Their great merit lies in the following qualities :—

" *Pluck*.—Irish Terriers are remarkably good-tempered, and can be implicitly relied upon with children ; they have this peculiarity, that they often appear shy and timid, but their true nature soon flashes out on occasion. Some of the pluckiest I have owned have had this peculiarity of appearing often timid, such as the late Tanner, Sporter, Banshee, Belle, &c. It is almost superfluous to speak of Irish Terriers' pluck ; they are the Bull-terriers of the sister isle, fear is unknown to them ; they are not only plucky as a breed, but individually. It is their fear-nothing natures that make them so suitable for use against the larger vermin. There are too many instances of their pluck on record to enumerate

15

IRISH TERRIER.

them. Mr. W. Graham, writing in the *Live Stock Journal*, says: 'In disposition the Irish Terrier is very tractable, steady at work, and easily kept under command, compared with other breeds possessing the same amount of courage; I am sorry to say they are kept by some parties for fighting purposes. I once went to purchase pups, when the owner insisted upon me seeing the dam, a champion bitch (the Fly already spoken of), draw the badger before taking away my purchase; and I know a prize dog lately killed a badger before his hold could be removed. Again, I know a bitch puppy under nine months that killed the first cat she ever saw, and in a very short time.' Mr. Galloway writes: 'My Irish Terrier bitch (Eily O'Connor, by Sporter) jumped into the river Logan to retrieve in the month of January last, at which time the river was half frozen over, when my Retriever refused point-blank to go, although he saw the duck drop, and the said Retriever boasts of England's best blood by sire and dam.'

"*Rabbiting.*—Looking at them as workmen, rabbiting must first be mentioned. This is their special function, and there are few things I can imagine so enjoyable as a day's ferreting with a couple of Irish Terriers. Rely upon it, their quick noses never make a mistake; they never pass a burrow where a bunny lies, nor do they stop a second at an empty one; and once the ferret in, bolt the rabbit ever so rapidly, he'll not escape the attention of the wild Irishman waiting outside for him. It is marvellous the pace these dogs go; their action represents the level sweep of a thorough-bred, and their powerful hind legs propel them forward at an enormous rate. It is only when one sees them at full speed that one can understand the necessity for insisting upon their peculiar build. Hunting in the furze, they fear nothing, but boldly push in through brambles, pricks, &c., that would make a thin-skinned dog yell out with pain. At this work they are superior to the conventional Spaniel, who works too slowly and carefully, and his long, thick coat holds him often enough; but the short, hard jacket of the red Paddies is no impediment, and they work about with a dash and fervour enjoyable to witness. Again, see them working hedgerows; how assiduously and well! You would never want to use another breed.

"*Stamina.*—They will bear any amount of hard work and rough usage; constitution appears to never trouble them, they can give most breeds points for stamina. Mr. Graham says: 'As I work all my Terriers with ferrets, and require a good game dog, also a constitutionally strong one to work in winter for a whole day, and probably sit for hours in frost and cold should the ferrets lodge, I find no breed suits me nearly so well as Irish Terriers. They are more hardy, require less care, and are more free from disease than any other Terrier with which I am acquainted.'

"*Badger.*—At badger the Irish Terrier is not to be touched. No punishment frights them off, they will hold on till death.

"*Foxes.*—With regard to foxes, a well-known breeder writes: 'I have experience of five packs of Fox-hounds, and not one Terrier of any breed is kept in either kennel. When the varmint is earthed, some persons detach themselves from the crowd, and run to the nearest house where lives an Irish Terrier. They need not be trained nor specially bred; they will do the work if Irish Terriers proper, without tuition. In the winter of 1874, in the county Louth, I was at the killing of five foxes. From the meet, at 9 A.M., until 3 P.M. there were three of them earthed, and these were unearthed by two different Irish Terriers, one 10 lbs. and the other 27 lbs. weight. The pack was owned by Viscount Massareene and Ferrard."
I prefer to give these quotations, as they contain facts and not general remarks

"*Otters.*—Here the Irish Terrier is in his element, and all his qualities are brought into play—love of the water, nose, pluck, and stamina. I quote an authority on this subject, Mr. Robert Dunscombe of Mount Desert, who says : ' I have had the pleasure of hunting two different packs of Otter-hounds, the former belonging to Mr. Johnson of Hermitage, and the latter to the Earl of Bandon of Castle Bernard, with both of which packs *pure-bred* Irish Terriers were used. I owned one, called Dandy, who would go to ground, challenge and bolt the largest otter out of any sewer, no matter how long or how wet. He, poor fellow, was poisoned by accident. This dog ran with Mr. Johnson's hounds, which were sold some years since. My present Terrier " Jessie," a pure Irish-bred one, of a light yellow colour, was given to me by a poor countryman, and her equal I never saw anywhere. She has bolted otters innumerable, and has always shown extraordinary gameness. I may mention as a proof of her pluck that during a capital hunt with Lord Bandon's hounds some weeks since, while the otter was being pressed from place to place by the hounds, Jessie, winding him under a bush, dived under water and laid hold of him ; after a severe struggle she came to the surface half drowned, being badly bitten across the loins. The otter when killed weighed 20 lbs.'

" *Water.*—I had Sporter and Moya Doolan hunting the creeks in the marsh-land in Essex for water-rats ; and it was a pretty sight to see them, one each side, working the banks, uttering no sound, only showing their excitement by their agitated sterns. As the rats dropped into the water, the dogs dived in after them. The Irish Terrier is as fond of the water and takes it as readily as a Newfoundland, and one enthusiastic owner claims a forty-five minutes' swim for a dog of this breed belonging to him.

" *Rats.*—Irish Terriers deserve no praise for their ratting qualities ; it is pure instinct with them, they cannot help it, they rat as naturally as a bird flies. My Banshee II. killed her first rat with her milk teeth when she was only 12 weeks old. The following extract of a letter from Mr. Ridgway speaks for their ratting capabilities and intelligence : ' An incident which I think speaks volumes for the sagacity and wisdom of the old Irish Terrier breed, was written to me lately by a gentleman residing in the County Antrim (north of Ireland, where, I may add, I believe some very fine specimens exist, from all I hear), and it was regarding the performance of a bitch of this breed, named Jess, in his possession. On one occasion we were boring a bank for the purpose of bolting rats, and at one place a rat bolted. Jess, as usual, had him almost before he cleared his hole. Then came another and another, so fast that the work was getting too hot for Jess, when a happy thought seemed to strike her ; and while in the act of killing a very big one, she leaned down her shoulder against the hole, and let them out one by one, until she had killed eighteen rats. That Irish Terriers kill neatly I cannot say ; they kill not wisely, but too well. Your little Black-and-tan shakes the life out of the rat ; but the Irish Terrier's jaw is so powerful, he doesn't need to shake, but crunches them into purgatory. They always impress me with the idea that the game is not big enough for them, and they put too much energy in it.'

" I consulted with Mr. Geo. Jamison, and the following scale of points on the whole fairly represents the opinions of us both :—

" *Head.*—Long ; skull flat, and rather narrow between ears, getting slightly narrower towards the eye ; free from wrinkle. Stop hardly visible, except in the profile. The jaw must be strong and muscular, but not too full in the cheek, and of a good punishing length, but not so fine as a white English Terrier's. There should be a slight falling away below the eye, so as not to have a Greyhound appearance.

"*Teeth.*—Should be strong and level.

"*Lips.*—Not so tight as a bull-terrier's, but well-fitting, showing through hair their black lining.

"*Nose.*—Must be black.

"*Eyes.*—A dark hazel colour, small, not prominent, and full of life, fire, and intelligence.

"*Ears.*—Small and V-shaped, of moderate thickness, set well up on the head, and dropping forward closely to the cheek. The ear must be free of fringe, and the hair thereon shorter and generally darker in colour than the body. Until some decided action be taken against it, we are afraid cropping will prevail, for it undoubtedly imparts a smart appearance to a dog, thus giving it an unfair and unnatural advantage over an uncropped dog. In the days when Irish Terriers were used as fighting dogs, it was reasonable and advisable to crop them ; but now that they are used only as working Terriers, we should not deprive them of the protection nature has given them, and which they must so sorely stand in need of when under earth or in the water. A cropped dog should not be qualified to score any points for ears. Good ears must be bred for. Hair on face, of same description as on body, but short (about a quarter of an inch long), in appearance almost smooth, and straight. A slight beard is the only longish hair (and it is only long in comparison with the rest) that is permissible, and that is characteristic.

"*Neck.*—Should be of a fair length, and gradually widening towards the shoulders, well carried, and free of throatiness.

"*Shoulders and Chest.*—Shoulders must be fine, long, and sloping well into the back ; the chest deep and muscular, but neither full nor wide.

"*Back and Loin.*—Body moderately long ; back should be strong and straight, with no appearance of slackness behind the shoulders ; the loin broad and powerful, and slightly arched, ribs well sprung, and well ribbed back.

"*The Hind Quarters.*—Well under the dog ; should be strong and muscular, the thighs powerful, hocks near the ground, stifles not much bent.

"*Stern.*—Invariably docked ; should be free of fringe or feather, set on pretty high, carried gaily, but not over the back, or curled.

"*Feet and Legs.*—Feet should be strong, tolerably round, and moderately small ; toes arched, and neither turned out nor in ; black toe-nails are preferable and desirable. Legs moderately long, well set from the shoulders, perfectly straight, with plenty of bone and muscle ; the elbows working freely clear of the sides, pasterns short and straight, hardly noticeable. Both fore and hind legs should be moved straight forward when travelling ; the stifles not turned outwards, the legs free of feather, and covered, like the head, with a hard texture of coat—as body, but not so long.

"*Coat.*—Hard and wiry, free of softness or silkiness, not so long as to hide the outlines of the body, particularly in the hind quarters, straight and flat, no shagginess, and free of lock or curl.

"*Colour.*—Must be 'whole-coloured,' the most preferable being bright red, next yellow, wheaten, and grey. White objectionable. It often appears on chest and feet ; it is more objectionable on the latter than on chest, as a speck of white on chest is frequently to be seen in all self-coloured breeds.

"*Size and Symmetry.*—Weight in show condition, from 16 to 24 lbs.—say 16 to 22 for bitches and 18 to 24 for dogs. The most desirable weight is 22 lbs. or under, which is a nice stylish and useful size. The dog must present a gay, lively, and active appearance ; lots of substance, at same time free of clumsiness, as speed and endurance, as well as power, are very essential. There must be a 'racing build' about the Irish Terrier.

"Disqualifying Points.—Nose white, cherry, or spotted to any considerable extent; mouth much undershot or cankered; colour brindle or very much white; coat much curly or very soft.

MR. GEORGE KREHL'S POINTS FOR JUDGING IRISH TERRIERS.

Head	15
Ears	5
Neck	5
Shoulders and chest	10
Back, loin, and stern (including general make of body)	15
Hind quarters	5
Feet and legs	15
Coat	15
Colour .. .. , ...	10
Size	5
Total	100 "

The subject of our coloured plate is the well-known and very successful dog Sporter, the property of Mr. George R. Krehl. This dog was formerly the property of Messrs. Despard and Graham. Amongst his chief performances are: 1st, Dublin; 1st and cup, Newtownards; 1st, Londonderry, 1878. He measures, from nose to stop, 2¾ inches; from stop to occiput, 4¼ inches; length of back, 14½ inches; girth of muzzle, 10 inches; girth of skull, 13 inches; girth of neck, 12 inches; girth round brisket, 22 inches; girth round shoulders, 25 inches; girth of loins, 15½ inches; girth of thigh, 10 inches; girth of forearm, 5½ inches; girth of pastern, 3½ inches; height at shoulders, 16 inches; height at elbows, 9 inches; height at loins, 16 inches; height, hock to ground, 4¾ inches. His age is about 4 years, and his weight 22 lbs.

The following scale agrees in all points with Mr. Krehl's enumeration—reduced, however, to simpler form, in accordance with the plan adopted throughout this work:—

POINTS OF IRISH TERRIERS.

Head and ears	10
Coat and colour	10
Legs and feet	10
Back and loin	5
Hind quarters and stern	5
Shoulders, neck, and chest	10
Total	50

THE IRISH TERRIER.

"THE Irish terrier is a cheap dog, is it not?" said a friend to me the other day. "I do not know about its cheapness," I replied; "but if you have a really good one it will bring a hundred pounds any time you want to sell it." And such is the fact. A first-class Irish terrier is worth almost as much as a fox terrier, and as a so-called marketable canine commodity ranks only after the latter, the collie, and the St. Bernard in value. He is a favourite dog, hence his worth.

His popularity has only come about during the past fifteen years or so; dog shows have been his fortune, and the Irish Terrier Club has no doubt assisted him to his high position. It was as far back as about 1882 that I was judging dogs at Belfast, and was then very much struck with the extraordinary character possessed by sundry Irish terriers which were brought into the ring; they included Mr. J. N. R. Pim's Erin, perhaps the best all-round specimen of her race that ever lived, her progeny Poppy and Playboy, and there were several other typical terriers whose names do not occur to me. I became enamoured of the variety, and then prognosticated a popular future for them should they only breed fairly true to character and type, and be produced with ears that did not require cutting. That I was not far wrong is plainly in evidence, as the Irish terrier must certainly be placed as the second terrier in popularity at the time I write.

The early volumes of the " Kennel Club Stud Book" did not contain special classes for Irish terriers, they being grouped with the wire-haired fox terriers. However, in 1876 they had a division for themselves, in which there were nineteen entries, five of which were owned by Mr. G. Jameson, of New-townards. To prove how the variety has increased since then, attention need only be called to the two hundred and twenty names of Irish terriers that appear in the most recent volume of the Stud Book, published in 1893. In 1878 and 1879 Birmingham first arranged classes for Irish terriers, and in the latter year, when there were fifteen entries, Messrs. Carey, W. Graham, A. Krehl, and G. R. Krehl were amongst the exhibitors in the two divisions provided.

Before the dates named we look in vain for classes for Irish terriers at the leading shows out of

Ireland. Such dogs were then, excepting by a few persons who knew them and kept them in their native country, considered mongrels, and so no doubt they would have continued had not their gameness and general excellence been suddenly discovered by the general public. That they are admirable companions cannot be denied, and one I have in the house now, a relative of champions, and by no means a bad-looking dog himself, is about as perfect a specimen of a dog of the London suburbs as can be imagined. But perhaps more of him anon, and any further remarks of my own shall be preceded by the opinions of one or two gentlemen who have given more attention to the Irish terrier than I could possibly have done, but that they are more ardent admirers of him I will not allow.

Mr. W. J. Cotton, of Blessington, co. Wicklow, who has bred and kept Irish terriers for a great number of years, writes characteristically of their origin as follows :

"To Sir Walter Raleigh, through potato skins, the Irish cottier, and hardships, we owe the Irish terrier. When Ireland was more thickly inhabited, there were small parties of cottiers grouped together ; each had his cabbage and potato garden badly fenced, and each family spent the greater portion of their time round the turf hearth, watching the murphies boil. The circle was incomplete, and liable to be disturbed in their beloved indolence, without a dog, which was hissed on when the neighbouring pig or goat invaded the boundary of the estate. A large dog required too much support ; one with some spice of pluck was, however, required in order to enforce its authority. The combination of Pat, pig, and potatoes, was conducive of rats— and rats of sport and rivalry. As such terriers were indiscriminately bred, and all ran wild, the dog with the most pluck exercised the largest influence on the breed.

"We can thus imagine the pups bearing the greatest resemblance to any particular champion were selected ; hence in this respect the survival of the fittest. During the day, as described, these terriers lay at the fire, and at night, though the pig might be given a corner of the cabin, the terrier was shown the outside of the door to guard the larder, which was the potato pit, look after the general safety of the estate, and to find a bed in the ditch or butt of the haycock. Generations of this treatment developed them into the 'pine knots' they are.

" Driving along the roads any hour of the night, this state of things you will find still to exist, and it is a matter of wonder how the inmates sleep and quite ignore the choruses of howls on moonlight nights. I believe myself that the Irish garrisons distributed over the country the bulldog, which was used for crossing. As many native fanciers say, to this day, there is nothing like a " cras " of the bull, and I think the Irish terriers' disposition largely shows it. You find them still of all types, long in leg, short on leg, and long in body, and crooked in legs, and of all colours, red, black, blue, brindle, and those with tan legs often have the best coats. I know at the present time brindles showing more of the modern type as regards length of leg and general conformation than the other colours.

"There is a glen, Imaal, in the Wicklow mountains that has always been, and still is, justly celebrated for its terriers. It would be hard to specify their colour in particular—the wheaten in all shades to that of bright red. In Kerry I think the black blue is most prevalent; quite black very uncommon, and I hardly ever saw a good specimen that colour. Mr. Chas. Galway, of Waterford, the breeder of the celebrated greyhound Master McGrath, for years, long before the Irish terrier came into fashion, always kept and bred the variety, and I am told there was no getting one from him. I am also informed the coats of his terriers were rather inclined to curl, and that the dogs themselves were undeniably game.

" The father of the present pedigree family was Killiney Boy, bred by Mr. Burke, of Queen's-street, Dublin. He passed from him to a Mr. Flannigan, residing at Castlenock, which place was purchased by Mr. Donnegan, Dane-street, Dublin, who found Killiney Boy running about deserted. The dog was duly adopted, and afterwards given to Mr. Howard Waterhouse, with whom he died a short time ago ; his dam was a rough black and tan bitch, the type now accepted as the Welsh terrier, hence the black and tan puppies so often found in the strains descended from him." It has been said that Killiney Boy was worried and almost eaten by a litter of puppies of which he was the sire.

Mr. C. J. Barnett, of Hambleden, whose name is a household word in connection with Irish terriers, says : " There is no doubt that the Irish terrier was the common terrier of Ireland a century ago, and is to this day the friend and companion of the native. Before railways were introduced, inter-breeding in certain localities caused a type which might have varied slightly in different districts, and as colour was a minor consideration, we so often find puppies even to the present day black and tan, grey or brindle in colour. This does not show bad breeding, but rather the contrary, to continue the colour through so many generations, for these dogs, like the Welsh ponies, no matter whatever they are crossed with, appear to perpetuate their peculiar characteristics. I have heard it stated that the pure Irishman was originally a large terrier, and to reduce the size a cross with a Manchester terrier was used, hence the black and tan puppies that are so often produced.

" I am happy to say I cannot find the slightest foundation for this statement ; I have myself tried such a cross carefully and it quite failed, and I am convinced it would take years to breed out the black and tan strain, with its sleek coat, and get back to the somewhat rugged outline and water-proof jacket of the Irish terrier.

" At an early Irish show, in 1874, there were classes given for Irish terriers under 9lb. weight, clearly showing that small terriers were fashionable then. In my rambles through Ireland I have generally asked for the man who kept the best terriers in the village, and, on hearing where he was, I went to see his dogs. He was always anxious to show me not only his own but those of his neighbours as well. I have seen good terriers which would get a prize at many of our English shows, but which were kept so out of sight, partly through fear of the ' corner boys,' that resident fanciers who regularly show were ignorant of their existence. These were owned by cottiers in the small towns and villages. I noticed that the majority of such dogs had a few grey or black hairs in their coats, but as a rule they were inclined to be a light red in colour and very hard in texture ; the ears are also larger as a rule than is fashionable in England, but well carried.

" At a small public house near Sion Mills, Strabane, is an Irish terrier dog, now 16 years of age, not at all the fashionable type, as he is very low on the leg and rather thick in front, but he has a charming head, with a most intelligent expression, and a good pair of ears. Wherever the Irish terrier may have got his type, there is no denying his real native expression and general characteristics, which have made him so popular in England.

" The foundations of the present generation of show terriers are nearly all descended from Mr. Waterhouse's Killiney Boy, and it is a difficult matter to find one that has not some drop of his blood in his veins. The red or yellow are now considered the correct colour, and the dark puppies are usually destroyed, but as the dam of Killiney Boy was a rough black and tan, colour is merely a question of fashion. When red puppies are born in the same litter as black and tans, the former are nearly always a good bright red ; but the black and tan have the better coats, invariably as hard as pin wire. I am by no means certain that by not using the latter to breed from we are losing the hard, wiry coats, and brighter red colour; and were it not for the art of trimming many of our winning terriers would have coats almost as shaggy as are found on some mountain sheep.

"When Irish terriers were first shown it was the fashion to crop their ears to a point, making them look very sharp. As they were often used as fighting dogs in the good old days, this might have been of some service, but of late years a strong feeling has grown up against it, and acting on the advice of the Irish Terrier Club, the Kennel Club passed a rule that no cropped Irish terrier born since Dec. 31, 1889, can compete at shows under their rules.

"Although nearly all our best terriers are, as already stated, descended from Killiney Boy, many trace their pedigree back to a union of that dog with a bitch named Erin, bought by Mr. W. Graham, of Belfast, before being shown at Dublin in 1879. This bitch was perhaps the best Irish terrier ever seen, and I very much doubt if any terrier of to-day is her superior, if her equal. Both Killiney Boy and Erin were cropped, but in their first litter there was a puppy born whose ears were so good that they were allowed to remain as nature made them. This puppy was afterwards named Play Boy; the others in the litter were Poppy, Pagan II., Gerald, Pretty Lass, with Peggy, who later was dam of Garryford. This must be acknowledged as a most extraordinary litter, and such a one has seldom been produced at one time.

" Erin was afterwards mated with another dog named Paddy II., and Garryowen and Glory were two of their puppies, and a bitch named Jess, who, put to Killiney Boy, threw a dog called Gripper. The latter was not successful at the stud, and bitches by him when put to dogs by either Killiney Boy or dogs descended from him, are very apt to throw black and tan, brindle, or grey.

" Of the earlier terriers none came up to Erin, who, bar her feet and cropped ears, was nearly perfect, and, until her own celebrated litter, was unrivalled. Mr. W. Graham, Newtownbreda, who has bred and owned a large number of winners, and is one of the leading authorities on the variety, is of opinion that she was the best Irish terrier he has yet seen.

" The competition between the brother and sister, Play Boy and Poppy, was always very keen, the bitch being cropped ; but the dog carried a pair of beautiful ears. Poppy was the richer in colour, and when young had a very keen and intelligent expression. Play Boy possessed the more substance, but his eyes were somewhat too full, which made him look somewhat quiet and hardly sharp enough.

" Play Boy was not a success at the stud, though he sired a dog named Bogie Rattler, owned by myself, who took after him in looks and good ears, but was lower on the leg, more cloddy, and not of Play Boy's quality. Bogie mated with Biddy III., by Gripper and Cora (drop ears), produced first Champion Bachelor, and, in the next litter, Benedict, which I sold to Mr. Graham. Benedict became the most celebrated stud dog of the day, for he is sire or grandsire of more winners than any other Irish terrier.

" Bachelor was very successful in the show ring, and took after his sire and grandsire in having a good pair of ears. He had also a very hard coat, of good colour, yellow tipped with red, a long neck, which was very muscular, and a well-shaped head, which never grew too thick ; his hind quarters were rather short, and his shoulders somewhat coarse, the latter no doubt caused by the amount of work he did. Benedict was a darker colour, with a lot of coat on his fore quarters, but little on his loins or hind quarters, and of rather a lighter make than Bachelor. It may interest my readers to know that in the litter which included Bachelor there were three red, one grey, and five rough black and tan coloured puppies, and in that in which Benedict was produced, there were three red and five rough black and tan in hue.

" A noted rival of Bachelor's on the show bench was Mr. Graham's Extreme Carelessness (afterwards sold to Mr. Graves, of Liverpool), a bitch that when a puppy was almost black, or rather, nearly every hair was more black than yellow. At four years of age the tips of a few hairs only were black, and two years ago, just before she died, I saw the old bitch in Ireland, looking very fit and well, but of a beautiful yellow-red colour, and entirely free from any black tinge. She was given back to Mr. Graham after she had finished her show career. Extreme Carelessness was cropped, her head rather heavy, and she had a slight slackness behind the shoulders, otherwise she was a charming bitch of great character and of good quality. She and Bachelor had many hard struggles for ' specials,' their successes being about equal.

" Erin, two years after her celebrated litter, again visited Killiney Boy, and threw a bitch, Droleen, who, put to a long-headed dog named Michael, by Pagan II., a grandson of both Killiney Boy and Erin, threw for her owner, Mr. E. A. Wiener, the best dog since Bachelor's days, Brickbat by name, who has had a most successful show career, winning the Challenge Cup given by the Irish Terrier Club twelve times, without once being defeated, and finally he secured it outright.

"Brickbat is unfortunately cropped, and his expression requires greater smartness; he is rather too big, and has a mere apology of a stern. Otherwise this excellent terrier is pretty nearly perfect.

"Poppy, to the best of my recollection, only bred one good puppy, called Poppy II., very like her dam, but of a lighter build, and too leggy. I think the above a rough outline of the earlier generation of Irish terriers, bringing them down to the present time, for, although Brickbat has retired from the show bench, he is still alive and vigorous, and in Mr. Wardle's studio the other day he looked quite fresh as he was standing for his picture.

"Although so popular on the show bench, it is as a companion that the Irish terrier has won his way into the hearts of those who own a dog for the house and to keep down vermin. I am glad to say that the show bench has not yet spoiled their good qualities; although many are 'kennel fools,' this is their misfortune, not their fault. I have entered my terriers to all kinds of vermin, except otter, at that they have not had the chance; but one small terrier, bred by a friend from my dogs and given to Mr. Harry Clift, when hunting the otter hounds he kept at Newbury, Berks, was one of the gamest little terriers he ever owned, almost too keen, and quite fearless.

" I remember turning out a badger to see if Bachelor, when he was under a year old, would seize and hold it.   At first they fought until almost tired out, then the dog got the badger by the cheek and there held him until they were both quite exhausted. The badger earths in our Buckinghamshire chalk hills are not large, but run very deep, often 16ft. to 18ft., so one cannot dig, and it is little short of cruelty to put a terrier in, as he may get blocked; it is too deep to hear a sound, and Irish terriers are not noisy enough, fighting and taking their punishment in silence, nor do they ' bay ' their game like other terriers.   I have often run two of my terriers, Boundary and Birthright, into small earths, and found them of no use, as we could not hear where they were, unless the badger grunted or they whined, and they have come out fearfully mauled and bitten.

" I accounted for one fox with an Irish terrier, and this was by accident, as I did not think the dog would kill it in less than half a minute or so, but he rolled it over, bit it through the brisket, and the fox was dead before I had time to get the dog off.

" It is in the water that Irish terriers excel, as they take to it as naturally as a duck, and as a rule retrieve well therefrom. I have a bitch that will dive many yards after a rat, or rather run in shallow water with her head under, trying to grab it. She will also, if about to kill in the river and the rat dives, dive under and kill; but often she has to leave go and come up for breath, when the rat sinks. In clear water I have seen her do this, and afterwards get the rat up, so there is no doubt she often kills under water.

"My terriers sometimes spend a day in digging out a rat; they go in hammer and tongs, and make a great show of having it out at once, but there is a method in their madness, as they keep an eye on the bolt holes, and after a vigorous scratch, jump up every now and then to see if the rat is trying to escape at the holes either above ground or those below the water line.

"The Irish terrier is of little use in rabbit shooting; it is dangerous for the dogs, as they are too near the same colour as the rabbit, and as a rule run mute. I myself have more than once put up the gun at one of the terriers, mistaking it for a hare. They are also too large to penetrate the rabbit runs in the brambles, and the meuses in our white-thorn laid hedgerows often check them. I have killed ten couples in a day by blocking the holes up and hunting the rabbits down. Irish terriers are keen enough and dead game, try their hardest to kill, but much as I love them I am compelled to say that they are not so good for rabbiting as beagles or small fox terriers, chiefly on account of their size and colour.

" I have seen it stated that an Irish terrier could catch a hare ; so it perhaps might if the hare had a trap to a leg, or was sick and poorly, but as there are some hares that a greyhound cannot kill on their own ground, it is not likely an Irish terrier could run down even an ordinary hare. Nor is it part of his duty to do so. Here is an account of a trial or two between an Irish terrier and a fox terrier noted for its skill in rabbit coursing :

" We slipped them in a stubble field. Just at the end the hare stopped to pick her run, and was out of sight when the terrier got through. The next slip was on a fallow, the hare having about ten yards start, at the end of the field there was a considerable slope up-hill. After ' puss ' had got about 150 yards ahead, we saw her look round and wait until the terriers got to within a yard or so, and then jump on one side and quietly jog away out of sight.

" I do not know a better companion for the man or woman who only keeps one dog than an Irish terrier, as he is easily trained, and in the house is most affectionate and thoroughly cleanly. To see him play with children, or guard them, is a pleasure. I have had some scores of Irish terriers, and I never yet saw one turn on or snap at a child. I had six out with me one day, and called at a friend's house where a children's party was being held. The dogs ran on the tennis lawn, and the little ones caught them and rolled them over. One dog, recently bought, had always been kennelled until he came to me, so I was afraid he might resent being pulled about, as he was of rather a quick temper, but to my surprise he enjoyed the romp, which was more than some of the mothers of the children did."

Mr. Barnett does not allude at length to the natural tendency some of the Irish terriers have to retrieve and fetch and carry. Barney, my dog in the house at Brixton, is never happier than when bringing the daily paper into the sitting-room from downstairs, where the boy has left it. A curious habit, too, he has. He may be waiting at the gate, and, seeing me in the distance, he will pick up any little piece of newspaper he finds in the roadway, and fetch it, though a mere scrap, but brought so tenderly between the lips as to leave not the slightest mark or dampness.

Barney, however, excelled himself one day when he brought into the house a teacup containing an egg. The former was carried by the rim, and carefully deposited into the hands of my house-keeper, the egg uncracked, the feat a record. One of the neighbours had given them to the dog, who evidently thought he could not do better with the presents than hand them over to his best friend. He was never trained to retrieve and fetch and carry ; the accomplishment is a natural one.

I can also speak personally of the capabilities of the Irish terrier as a water dog, for I have seen puppies at four months old swim across a strong stream fifty yards wide, follow the older ones hunting, and as keen "on rats" as the fully grown dogs could possibly be. These juveniles would also kill rabbits, and generally their precocity was quite astonishing. But it must be borne in mind that these young "Irishmen" had not been reared in kennels, they, on the contrary, having a free range in which to play, and where they could hunt either rats or rabbits when so inclined.

Mention may be made here of an Irish terrier who, perhaps, rejoiced in the name of Rags. Anyhow, he was a performer on the stage, his great feat being turning somersaults, which he did backwards, and, as a variety, turned "double somersaults," the latter

I fancy about as difficult a feat as any dog ever attempted and performed successfully.

Before proceeding to the description and points of the Irish terrier, the following notes by Mr. W. C. Bennett, of Dublin, will perhaps be interesting, although they go over much the same ground as that which we have already traversed.

" From what I have been able to gather from those who, like myself, are interested in this variety of the canine·race, and from what I can recall of early specimens, I have come to the conclusion that the present show terriers are a more or less ' made up ' breed, though doubtless a variety of terrier existed, resembling the present dogs, somewhat as a half-bred filly resembles a thoroughbred mare.

" My first recollection of the breed dates back some thirty years, to a brace of bitches owned by a relative residing in Parsonstown, who procured them from a trainer on the Curragh. They were high on the leg, somewhat open in coat, and wheaten in colour, and this latter is, I have always considered, the proper shade for the jacket of any Irish terrier. Most of the earlier specimens exhibited were of this hue, the bright red now, or recently, so fashionable being almost unknown. About the same time, or a few years later perhaps, I made the acquaintance of a rare old stamp of bitch, which was brought from the North of Ireland, and many a day's outing we had together; she was harder and closer in coat than those mentioned above, coloured bright wheaten, and nearer in shape and character, and in all respects, to the present show type than anything else I saw at that period.

" Few people in those early days gave much attention to the appearance of their terriers, and if they were game, and good at destroying rats and other vermin, they would be kept and bred from, and as these terriers were principally owned by farmers and cottiers, who kept one or two roaming about their houses and farms, they were hardly likely to be very select in the matter of breeding. Even to this day, in parts of the country, one comes across this old breed, as often as not with tails undocked, and sometimes, alas, showing a dash of greyhound blood. Many of them, too, are brindled in colour, and certainly smart terrier-like animals.

" I have several times been assured by those from whom I sought information, that a special strain of Irish terriers was kept in their families for generations, and they usually described them as wheaten coloured, open coated, with long, punishing jaws, and I was shown by a friend of mine (lately deceased) a game-looking wheaten coloured bitch, long and low on the leg, with a very open coat, long, level head, with little or no stop visible. The owner claimed to have had her breed for over thirty years in his family. I can vouch that she would fight until nearly killed, if once provoked.

" County Wicklow lays claim to a breed of what were so-called Irish terriers ; they frequently showed a blue shade on the back, were long in body, and rather short on leg, and even so recently as the year 1887 a class was given at the show held in Limerick, for silver-haired Irish terriers, the specimens exhibited being a slate blue colour. They were not to my mind a distinct variety, nor very terrier-like in appearance, and I believe the difficulty in getting a uniformity of type when breeding from the very best blood obtainable is proof positive that more than one strain was used in producing the present fashionable dog.

" In the first collection I saw in the Exhibition Palace Show, held in Dublin early in the seventies, there were scarcely two of the same size or weight exhibited, and with few, very few, exceptions they were a rough lot.

" Mr. P. Flanaghan, of Dublin, had many of the old sort, and game ones they were. He used them for badger drawing, and in the National Show alluded to, he exhibited a bitch, Daisy, which was described in the catalogue as 'well known to be of the purest and gamest breed in Ireland.' Mr. Cotton, of Blessington, also possesses terriers descended from stock for many years in his possession, and owned by him before classes were given at shows for them. His Cruisk (who won prizes in Dublin and elsewhere) is, however, as unlike the earlier sort as possible, as he is a neat terrier-like dog, with beautifully carried ears, and a hard, crisp coat — a charming dog brimful of character.

" I have seen and owned puppies by the celebrated Killiney Boy, and by dogs tracing from him, with short coats and black hairs. The old dog was open in coat, with a grand terrier head, straight in hocks, but a game little tyke, and died fighting—being killed in a kennel row. He had grown quite white in face and chest when last I saw him ; and many of his strain, earlier in life than is the case with most other dogs (like the Palmerston strain of Irish setters), grow grizzled about the head.

" A glance at the pedigree of almost any of the noted winners of the day will serve to show how much Killiney Boy did to bring the breed to its present form, as few pedigrees are without his name, and many of them on both sire and dam side trace back to him. Curiously enough, the short-haired mahogany-coloured specimens often prove very serviceable when bred from, and throw pups with plenty of coat, and this I have proved myself, and heard other breeders assert. Mr. Barnett's Benedict (brother to Champion Bachelor) was a notable instance of this, being very short in coat on body and sides, and he probably got as many winners on the bench as any dog of this variety.

"The north of Ireland was the stronghold of the Irish terriers for many a day, and still holds its own, with Mr. William Graham to aid it. Even there I should doubt if a pure descent of Irish terrier could be traced back for thirty years, as so long ago no one cared to go to the trouble of breeding them to one uniform type, and those who used them for fighting purposes crossed them with the bull terrier to increase their gameness and punishing power.

"Wexford, Dublin, and other parts had strains of their own, and when classes were formed at shows, and good prizes offered, fair specimens of the old sort were to be had, which, with judicious mating, produced a level and neat terrier, but these, as before observed, frequently threw back to the old stock, and sometimes a rough, open coated puppy still appears in the best bred litters, differing from all his brothers and sisters. Strange to say the freedom from stop, which is one of the characteristics of the present dog, was highly thought of in the dogs bred in former days, and as the ears were almost invariably cropped it mattered little how they came, but if uncut were usually heavy and carried low on the head.

"A glance at the earlier show catalogues confirms what I have written above as to the doubtful breeding of the earlier terriers.

"Take the Exhibition Palace Show at Dublin in 1874. Here classes were divided as 'dogs and bitches exceeding 9lb., and dogs and bitches under that weight;' in the former class ten competed, and half that number had no pedigree assigned to them; in the latter class only three competed, one of these, the second prize winner, having no pedigree. The following year three classes were provided, including a champion class 'for winners of a first prize at any show.' Dogs over 9lb. and bitches over 9lb. Four champions (save the mark) competed; two had pedigrees and the other two had none. In dogs over 9lb. six competed, two only having pedigrees. Four bitches over 9lb. were entered, half that number having pedigrees and half not.

"At the Dublin show in 1878 there were even fewer competitors, a dog and bitch class being given, with no restrictions as to weight. In the former there were four entries, and in the latter three, but only two of the lot appear to be able to boast of a pedigree.

" Does not the above prove that pedigrees in those days were little attended to, otherwise surely they would be stated if known. Some of the entries in these old catalogues are amusing, one entry being described as ' Pedigree terrier, well bred ; ' another, appropriately named ' The Limb, this bitch has jumped off all the highest bridges in and about Dublin.' Needless to say she was entered as ' not for sale.' ' Jack ' appears to have been a favourite name, and three with this cognomen competed in one class, and, oh, ' the grumbling ' at the awards, for everyone thought his tyke the only true and only genuine article, and owners were by no means loth to express their opinions in words."

A year or so later good ones appeared, such as Messrs. Carey's Sport, Spuds, and Sting, Mr. Waterhouse's Killiney Boy, and Mr. Wm. Graham's Erin, the latter brace when mated producing such good ones as Pagan II. and Play Boy, the particulars of which are fully given in what Mr. Barnett has contributed earlier on.

Some of the best Irish terriers have already been

mentioned, but omission should not be made of dogs so good as Gripper; Major Arnand's Fury II.; Phadruig; Dr. Carey's Sting; Peter Bodger (Mr. Waterhouse); Mr. H. A. Graves' Glory (the smallest Irish terrier that attained champion honours); Mr. W. Graham's Gilford; Mr. Backhouse's Buster, Bumptious Biddy, and Begum; Nora Tatters, a great favourite of mine, with Droleen and Bencher, all Mr. Wiener's; Mr. Sumner's St. George and B.A.; Dan'el II., Breadenhill; Mr. F. Breakell's Bonnet; Mr. Mayell's Chaperon and Mr. A. E. Clear's Breda Mixer. Still another youngster that I opine will not be long in becoming a champion is Mr. C. J. Barnett's Black Sheep, a dog of 24lb. weight, about the size the best of them have been. His dark face may be objectionable, and he is perhaps a mere trifle long in back, but, all round, I have never seen a better terrier, and I fancy that, assisted by his excellent pair of natural ears, he will be the first dog to lower the colours of Mr. Wiener's so long successful Brickbat, if his owner has the temerity to place the latter on the bench again.

Another favourite Irish terrier of mine is Mr. Barnett's Birthright. She weighs 18lb., and has been kept out of many prizes because some judges consider her small. Her character and general form are exquisite. Other typical Irish terriers up to date are Mrs. Butcher's Bawnboy and Ted Malone; Mr. T. Yarr's Poor Pat; Mr. F. Parkyn's Firefly; Mr. Jowett's Crowgill Sportsman; Mr. C. B. Murless's Magic; Mr. Krehl's Bishop's Boy; Mr. T. Wallace's Treasurer; whilst from time to time Mr. James Sumner, Mr. J. W. Taylor, Dr. Marsh, Mr. F. W. Jowett, Mr. H. Benner, Mr. C. R. Norton, Mr. C. M. Nicholson, and Mr. T. C. Tisdall, have all owned Irish terriers of more than ordinary excellence.

The Irish Terrier Club was established in 1879, and proving unusually liberal in supporting certain shows, has no doubt done much to popularise the variety over which it looks. Its challenge cup is valuable and handsome, which, as already stated, was won outright by Brickbat, but two cups of equal value will shortly be offered by the club.

Considerable difference of opinion has been expressed as to the description of the Irish terrier as issued by the club, it evidently being modelled on that of the fox terrier. The following, compiled by an " up to date " admirer and successful breeder of the variety, will give an idea of the " points " of an Irish terrier; at any rate, when assisted by Mr. Wardle's drawings, they will do so.

"*Head.*—Long and flat, not pinched or lumpy, and not too full in the cheek; showing but a very slight stop in profile. Jaw strong, of a punishing length and of good depth. A thin, weak jaw is objectionable, as is a short, thick head.

"*Teeth.*—Level, white, and sound ; both over or undershot objectionable and disqualifying.

"*Nose.*—Black.

"*Eyes.*—Brown, dark hazel, or black, the latter however, are apt to give the dog a curious expression. They should be small, keen, and more almond-shaped than round, set in the head and not on the head. Light eyes very objectionable.

"*Ears.*—Fairly thick, V-shaped, and set on to fall to the corner of the eye and close to the cheeks, but not at a right angle to the head ; they should not be set on too high or point to the nose.

"*Neck.* — Long, clean, and muscular, slightly arched, free from throatiness and nicely placed in the shoulders, not set on the top of them.

"*Shoulders.*—Strong and fine, nicely sloping to the back and firm to the hand, the dog should feel strong when pressed on the shoulders, the withers narrow, and gracefully joining the neck and back.

" *Chest.*—Of good depth, wide enough to give the heart and lungs free play, but not wide when viewed in front.

" *Back.*—Straight and strong.

" *Loin.*—Very slightly arched.

" *Stern.*—Docked or shortened, set rather high, must be gaily carried but not curled; the stern should be placed on in a line with the back, if too low it gives the dog a mean and unsymmetrical appearance behind.

" *Body.*—Of good depth, well ribbed up, but not too far back, or it will make him seem too thick-set and cobby, and detract from his appearance of liberty; flank slightly tucked up, but not enough to make the dog look shelly or light. Ribs inclined to flatness and not too much arched or sprung.

" *Legs and Feet.*—The legs should be strong, straight, and muscular, but not too upright in the pasterns, which should be slightly springy; elbows set strongly to the shoulders, moving freely, not tied too closely under him; the feet thick and hard, toes arched; open, long, or thin feet most objectionable.

" *Hind quarters.*—Very strong and muscular, long from hip to hock, not too wide but thick through, with no appearance of weakness, legs fairly under the dog, the hocks must move straight, cow hocks or hind legs bent outwards most objectionable.

"*Coat.*—Hard, straight, and wiry, free from silkiness anywhere; about 2½in. long on body, shorter on the head and ears, save a beard on the chin, short and hard on the legs, on no account curly; a soft, curly, or open coat objectionable.

"*Colour.*—Red-yellow, wheaten, or light brown inclining to grey; the best colour is orange tipped with red, the head slightly darker than the body, and the ears slightly darker than the head. The colour should not run out on the legs a dirty or dull dark red; a mahogany shade is objectionable.

"*Size.*—Height, dogs 16in. to 16½in., bitches 15½in. to 16in.; length from shoulder to set on of stern, dogs 14¾in. to 15¼in., bitches 14in. to 15in.; girth of chest, 20½in. to 21½in.; weight for dogs 20lb. to 24lb., bitches 18lb. to 22lb.

"*General appearance.*—The Irish terrier should appear to be of good constitution, somewhat rough in outlook, but thoroughly symmetrical. As the stern is high set on it gives the hind quarters a somewhat jumped-up look; the movements are rather jerky behind, as if the hind quarters possessed the power of moving quicker than the fore-end—almost a hare-like movement; the expression should be wicked, but intelligent, altogether a rough, merry, but game-looking terrier, not cobby nor too coarse.

" *Temperament.*—Temper very good, often shy, but always game. When at work, utterly without fear, and rather headstrong ; when in the house, quiet, affectionate, and loving. It is a characteristic of the Irish terrier to thrust his nose into his master's hand, or rest the head on his foot, or against his legs."

Positive Points.	Value.	Negative Points.	Value.
Head	10	White on toes or feet...	5
Teeth and eyes	10	Mouth undershot or overshot	20
Ears	10		
Neck	5	Very much white on chest	5
Legs and feet	15		
Chest and shoulders	10	Coat curly or soft	20
Back and loin and hind quarters	15		
Coat	10		
Colour	5		
General outline	10		
	100		50

DISQUALIFYING POINTS.

Brindled in colour, nose cherry or flesh-coloured; white legs—indeed any white, either on the feet, chest, or elsewhere, is objectionable. At four or five years old a few white hairs, giving a grizzly appearance about the muzzle, is not detrimental.

The following is the description issued by the Irish Terrier Club :

Positive Points.	Value.	Negative Points.		Value.
Head, jaw, teeth, and eyes	15	White nails, toes, and feet	minus	10
Ears	5	Much white on chest	,,	10
Legs and feet	10	Ears cropped	,,	5
Neck	5	Mouth undershot or cankered	,,	10
Shoulders and chest	10			
Back and loin	10	Coat shaggy, curly, or soft	,,	10
Hind quarters and stern	10	Uneven in colour	,,	5
Coat	15			
Colour	10			
Size and symmetry	10			
	100			**50**

Disqualifying Points : Nose cherry or red.   Brindle colour.

Descriptive Particulars.

" *Head.*—Long ; skull flat, and rather narrow between ears, getting slightly narrower towards the eye ; free from wrinkle ; stop hardly visible, except in profile. The jaw must be strong and muscular, but not too full in the cheek, and of a good punishing length, but not so fine as a white English terrier's. There should be a slight falling away below the eye, so as not to have a greyhound appearance. Hair on face of same description as on body, but short (about a quarter of an inch long), in appearance almost smooth and straight; a slight beard is the only longish hair (and it is only long in comparison with the rest) that is permissible, and that is characteristic.

"*Teeth*.—Should be strong and level.

"*Lips*.—Not so tight as a bull terrier's, but well-fitting, showing through the hair their black lining.

"*Nose*.—Must be black.

"*Eyes*.—A dark hazel colour, small, not prominent, and full of life, fire, and intelligence.

"*Ears*.—When uncut, small and V-shaped, of moderate thickness, set well up on the head, and dropping forward closely to the cheek. The ear must be free of fringe, and the hair thereon shorter and generally darker in colour than the body.

"*Neck*.—Should be of a fair length, and gradually widening towards the shoulders, well carried, and free of throatiness. There is generally a slight sort of frill visible at each side of the neck, running nearly to the corner of the ear, which is looked on as very characteristic.

"*Shoulders and Chest*.—Shoulders must be fine, long, and sloping well into the back; the chest deep and muscular, but neither full nor wide.

"*Back and Loin*.—Body moderately long; back should be strong and straight, with no appearance of slackness behind the shoulders; the loin broad and powerful and slightly arched; ribs fairly sprung, rather deep than round, and well ribbed back.

"*Hind Quarters.*—Well under the dog; should be strong and muscular, the thighs powerful, hocks near the ground, stifles not much bent.

"*Stern.*—Generally docked; should be free of fringe or feather, set on pretty high, carried gaily, but not over the back or curled.

Feet and Legs.—Feet should be strong, tolerably round, and moderately small; toes arched, and neither turned out nor in; black toe-nails are preferable and most desirable. Legs moderately long, well set from the shoulders, perfectly straight, with plenty of bone and muscle; the elbows working freely clear of the sides, pasterns short and straight, hardly noticeable. Both fore and hind legs should be moved straight forward when travelling, the stifles not turned outwards, the legs free of feather, and covered, like the head, with as hard a texture of coat as body, but not so long.

"*Coat.*—Hard and wiry, free of softness or silkiness, not so long as to hide the outlines of the body, particularly in the hindquarters, straight and flat, no shagginess, and free of lock or curl.

"*Colour.*—Should be 'whole-coloured,' the most preferable being bright red; next wheaten, yellow, and grey, brindle disqualifying. White sometimes appears on chest and feet ; it is more objectionable on the latter than on the chest, as a speck of white on chest is frequently to be seen in all self-coloured breeds.

"*Size and Symmetry.*—Weight in show condition, from 16lb. to 24lb.—say, 16lb. to 22lb. for bitches and 18lb. to 24lb. for dogs. The most desirable weight is 22lb. or under, which is a nice, stylish, and useful size. The dog must present an active, lively, lithe, and wiry appearance ; lots of substance, at the same time free of clumsiness, as speed and endurance, as well as power, are very essential. They must be neither ' cloddy ' nor ' cobby,' but should be framed on the ' lines of speed,' showing a graceful ' racing outline.'

"*Temperament.*—Dogs that are very game are usually surly or snappish. The Irish terrier, as a breed, is an exception, being remarkably good-tempered, notably so with mankind, it being admitted, however, that he is, perhaps, a little too ready to resent interference on the part of other dogs. There is a heedless, reckless pluck about the Irish terrier which is characteristic, and, coupled with the headlong dash, blind to all consequences, with which he rushes at his adversary, has earned for the breed the proud epithet of ' The Dare-Devils.' When ' off duty ' they are characterised by a quiet caress-inviting appearance, and when one sees them endearingly, timidly pushing their heads into their masters' hands it is difficult to realise that on occasion, at the 'set-on,' they can prove they have the courage of a lion, and will fight on to the last breath in their bodies. They develop an extraordinary devotion to, and have been known to track their masters almost incredible distances."

This "club description" has given rise to a considerable amount of controversy, but I believe it was drawn up by the leading admirers of the Irish terrier a few years ago, and if fault may be found with one or two of the items, such are of little importance so far as the general delineation of the dog is concerned. Unlike the Bedlington terrier, the Irish terrier is progressive so far as public estimation is concerned, and as I conclude this article I am told of a *bond-fide* offer of £220 for a couple of young dogs which have not yet been placed as the best of their variety.

W. J. Comstock's, Providence, R.
DUNMURRY.

THE TERRIER (IRISH).

ORIGIN.—Mr. George R. Krehl, editor of the London (England) "Stockkeeper" and English vice-president of the Irish Terrier Club, says this is a true and distinct breed, indigenous to Ireland, and that no man can trace its origin, which is lost in antiquity.

USES.—Rabbiting, and as a vermin-dog.

* SCALE OF POINTS, ETC.

	Value.		Value.
Head, jaws, teeth, and eyes .	15	Hind quarters and stern .	10
Ears	5	Coat	15
Legs and feet . . .	10	Color	10
Neck	5	Size and symmetry . .	10
Shoulders and chest . .	10		
Back and loins . . .	10	Total . . .	100

Negative Points.

White nails, toes, and feet .	10	Coat shaggy or curly . · .	10
Much white on chest . .	10	Uneven in color . . .	5
Ears cropped . . .	5		
Mouth undershot . .	10	Total . . .	50

HEAD.—Long; skull flat, rather narrow between ears, free from wrinkle; stop hardly visible. Jaws strong, muscular, but not too full in cheek, and of good punishing length. There should be a slight falling away below the eye, so as not to have a greyhound appearance. Hair on face same description as on body: short (about ¼ inch long), almost smooth and straight; a slight beard is permissible, and that is characteristic. Teeth strong and level. Lips not so tight as a bull-terrier's, but well fitting. Nose black. Eyes dark hazel, small, not prominent, full of life, fire, and intelligence. Ears, when uncut, small and V-shaped, of moderate thickness, set well up, dropping forward close to cheek, free from fringe, and hair thereon shorter and generally darker in color than the body.

NECK.—Fair length, gradually widening toward shoulders, free from throatiness, with a slight sort of frill at each side of neck, running nearly to corner of ear, which is characteristic.

SHOULDERS AND CHEST.—Shoulders *must* be fine, long, sloping; chest deep, muscular, but neither full nor wide.

BACK AND LOINS.—Body moderately long; back strong, straight, with no appearance of slackness; loins broad, powerful, slightly arched; ribs fairly sprung, rather deep than round.

HIND QUARTERS.—Well under the dog, strong, muscular; thighs powerful; hocks near the ground; stifles not much bent.

STERN.—Generally docked, free from fringe or feather; set on pretty high; carried gaily, but not over back, nor curled.

FEET AND LEGS.—Feet strong, tolerably round, moderately small; toes arched, neither turned out nor in; black toe-nails. Legs moderately long, well set on, perfectly straight, plenty of bone and muscle; pasterns short and straight; fore and hind legs moving straight forward when traveling; stifles not turned outward; legs free of feather, and covered with hair as on head.

COAT.—Hard, wiry, not soft nor silky, not so long as to hide outlines of body; straight, flat, no shagginess, no lock nor curl.

COLOR.—"Whole-colored," the most preferable being bright red, wheaten, yellow, and gray; *brindle disqualifying*. White sometimes appears on chest and feet; more objectionable on the latter.

SYMMETRY.—The dog must present an active, lively, lithe, and wiry appearance; lots of substance, free of clumsiness, and framed on the "lines of speed."

TEMPERAMENT.—The Irish terrier, as a breed, is remarkably good-tempered, notably so with mankind, it being admitted, however, that it is perhaps a little too ready to resent interference on part of other dogs, hence called "daredevils."

WEIGHT.—Sixteen to twenty-four pounds.

DISQUALIFICATIONS.

Nose cherry or red; brindle color.

Mr. H. T. Cousin's (Fenton Kennels, Salem, Mass.)
"FENTON PHADRUIG"

THE IRISH TERRIER

Origin.—Mr. George R. Krehl, editor of the London (England) "Stockkeeper" and English vice-president of the Irish Terrier Club, says that this is a true and distinct breed indigenous to Ireland, and that no man can trace its origin, which is lost in antiquity.

Uses.—Rabbiting and as a vermin dog.

*STANDARD.

Head.—Long, with skull flat and rather narrow between ears, getting slightly narrower towards the eye; free from wrinkle; with stop hardly visible, except in profile. Jaw strong and muscular, but not too full in the cheek, and of a good punishing length. There should be a slight falling away below the eye, so as not to have a Greyhound appearance. Hair on face of same description as on body, but short (about a quarter of an inch long), in appearance almost smooth and straight; a slight beard is the only longish hair (and it is long only in comparison with the rest) that is permissible, and that is characteristic.

Teeth.—Strong and level, lips not so tight as a Bull Terrier's, but well fitting, showing through the hair their black lining. Nose black.

Eyes.—Of a dark hazel color, small, and not prominent, and full of life, fire and intelligence.

Ears.—Small and V-shaped, of moderate thickness, set well on the head, and dropping forward closely to the cheek. The ear must be free of fringe, and the hair thereon shorter and darker in color than the body. No cropped Irish Terrier born since March 1, 1897, can compete for any prizes offered by the Club.

60

Neck.—Of a fair length, and gradually widening towards the shoulders, well carried, and free of throatiness. There is generally a slight sort of frill visible at each side of the neck, running nearly to the corner of the ear.

Shoulders and Chest.—Shoulders fine, long and sloping well into the back; chest deep and muscular, but neither full nor wide.

Feet and Legs.—Feet strong, tolerably round, and moderately small; toes arched, and neither turned out nor in; black toe-nails are most desirable. Legs moderately long, well set from the shoulders, perfectly straight, with plenty of bone and muscle; the elbows working freely clear of the sides; pasterns short and straight, hardly noticeable. Both fore and hind-legs should be moved straight forward when travelling, stifles not turned outwards, legs free of feather and covered like the head with as hard a texture of coat as body, but not so long.

Mrs. J. L. Kernochan's (Meadows Kennels, Hempstead, L. I.)
"RED GEM"

Back and Loins.—Body moderately long; back strong and straight; with no appearance of slackness behind the shoulders; loin broad and powerful and slightly arched; ribs fairly sprung, rather deep than round, and well ribbed back.

Hind-quarters.—Strong and muscular, the thighs powerful, hocks near the ground, stifles moderately bent.

Stern.—Generally docked; should be free of fringe or feather, but well covered with rough hair, set on pretty high, carried gaily but not over the back or curled.

61

Coat.—Hard and wiry, free of softness or silkiness, not so long as to hide the outlines of the body, particularly in the hind-quarters, straight and flat, no shagginess, and free of lock or curl.

Color.—Whole colored, the most preferable being bright red, red wheaten or yellow red. White sometimes appears on chest and feet; it is more objectionable on the latter than on the chest as a speck of white on chest is frequently seen in all self-colored breeds.

Size and Symmetry.—The most desirable weight in show condition is, for a dog 24 lbs., and for a bitch 22 lbs. The dog must present an active, lively, lithe, and wiry appearance; lots of substance, at the same time free of clumsiness, as speed and endurance, as well as power, are very essential. They must be neither cloddy nor cobby but should be framed on the lines of speed showing a graceful racing outline.

Temperament.—Dogs that are very game are usually surly or snappish. The Irish terrier, as a breed, is an exception, being remarkably good-tempered, notably so with mankind, it being admitted, however, that he is perhaps a little too ready to resent interference on the part of other dogs. There is a heedless, reckless pluck about the Irish terrier which is characteristic, and coupled with the headlong dash, blind to all consequences with which he rushes at his adversary, has earned for the breed the proud epithet of "The Dare-Devils." When "off duty" they are characterized by a quiet caress-inviting appearance, and when one sees them endearingly, timidly pushing their heads into their master's hands it is difficult to realize that on occasion, at the "set-on," they can prove they have the courage of a lion, and will fight on to the last breath in their bodies. They develop an extraordinary devotion to, and have been known to track their masters almost incredible distances.

*SCALE OF POINTS.

Head, ear and expression	20	Hind-quarters and stern	10
Legs and feet	15	Coat	15
Neck	5	Color	10
Shoulders and chest	10	Size and symmetry	10
Back and loins	5		
Total			100

*NEGATIVE POINTS.

White nails, toes and feet	10	Mouth undershot or cankered	10
Much white on chest	10	Coat shaggy, curly or soft	10
Dark shadings on face	5	Uneven in color	5
Total			50

COMMENTS.

The way in which the Irish terrier has grown in favor within the last few years has surprised even its most ardent admirers and he now bids fair to soon be able to try conclusions with the Fox terrier for general popularity. We have now some rare good ones here and among them are some that have been bred here too. If the faddist will only keep his "hands off" this breed we may hope soon to try our luck abroad in the show ring, and with a reasonable hope of success.

The head is one of the most charming features of this breed. One that is heavy in skull or weak before the eyes, cheeky, or showing a decided stop are faults that cannot be countenanced. A red or cherry colored nose is considered as disqualifying, though the standard does not so mention it, in fact it makes no reference to it at all in its "negative points." Light eyes are also generally considered very objectionable. Just at present some of the fanciers are up in arms concerning the "slight beard" question, which like similar subjects right themselves sooner or later. The sooner this one is settled the better, as the dog bears no relation to the goat except to hurry him up. All things considered equal, the cropped-eared dog forfeits five points to the one whose ears are shown as grown. As the Irish terrier is one of the fastest of terriers it will be readily seen that he should have good and well-placed legs and feet, sloping shoulders and strong back. Extremes of either length or shortness of back are equally objectionable. In the same category is placed an open or soft coat. The tail is set on high, which gives a peculiar appearance to the hind-quarters, and does not tend to make the dog's movements very graceful. In the matter of color, some good judges seem to think that brindle should disqualify a dog from at least winning the first prize, and the Irish Terrier Club on the other side says "brindle disqualifying."

The Irish terrier must be absolutely free of all lumber and must also be trim and racy in appearance, in fact, a terrier every inch of him. While every breeder should strive for bone, and plenty of it, yet it should not be so in evidence as to give the dog the appearance of clumsiness. A happy medium in this particular should be sought after and obtained.

The standard calls for the scoring of 15 points for the coat. Many an otherwise good dog has been "knocked down the line" for being deficient in this respect, failing in hardness and that wiry feeling which is so eagerly sought after. The high value (15) placed upon this quality shows how essential it is, and every breeder should look well over prospective stud-dogs, giving the preference, where all things are equal, to the one whose coat fills the requirements of the standard.

From photo by Rosemont, Leeds

MR. TOM ASHTON'S IRISH TERRIER LEEDS AMBASSADOR

From photo by Marsh Bros., Henley-on-Thames

MR. C. J. BARNETT'S IRISH TERRIERS

BOGIE RATTLER   BIDDY III. BENEDICT   CHAMPION   BRONZE
                                            BACHELOR

65

THE IRISH TERRIER

IT is certain that during the past two decades no breed of dog has attained greater popularity than the Irish Terrier, and a visit to any of our leading shows will be convincing proof of this, for in point of number he only plays second fiddle to his white relation the Fox-terrier, which has been a general favourite in England for generations past. The reason is not far to seek. Is it not a firm of soap-makers who say of their soap, " Once used, always used " ? Surely it would be difficult to find more appropriate words for the Irish Terrier. His genial disposition, all round merit for sport, racy outline, eyes that are teeming with kindness and intelligence peeping from underneath his shaggy old eyebrows, and a pin-wire, rusty horseshoe-coloured jacket that covers one of the biggest hearts that ever beat in a canine body, must command admiration from all who love a truly good, high-couraged Terrier.

It is a circumstance much to be regretted that the true origin of this grand Terrier has never come to light, and at this distant date in all probability it never will. We can therefore only accept the gleanings of those who have used their best efforts to solve the problem.

Mr. G. R. Krehl, the English Vice-President of the Irish Terrier Club, who has done so much this side of St. George's Channel to popularise Irish Terriers, in writing for Mr. Vero Shaw's book thus speaks of the breed :—

"The Irish Terrier is a true and distinct breed indigenous to Ireland, and no man can trace its origin, which is lost in antiquity. Mr. Ridgway, of Waterford, whose name is familiar in Irish Terrier circles from having drawn up the first code of points, states that they have been known to Ireland as long as that country has been an island, added to which there is the fact that there exist old manuscripts in Irish mentioning the breed at a very remote period. In old pictures representing scenes of Irish life an Irish Terrier or two are often to be descried.

Ballymena and County Wicklow may almost claim to be the birth-place of the breed. Most of the best specimens hail from Ballymena and the neighbourhood, where Mr. Thomas Erwin, of Irish Setter fame, boasts an extensive experience of this breed, and has always kept a few of the right old working sort for sporting purposes ; and in County Wicklow, Mr. Merry says, it is well known that the pure breed of Irish Terriers has been carefully kept distinct and highly prized for more than a century. Mr. E. F. Despard, whose name is well known in Irish Terrier circles as a very successful breeder and exhibitor, claims an acquaintance of over forty years with the breed. Mr. George Jamison, too, has known and kept them many years, and up till a little while ago had won more prizes than all the rest of the breeders put together. These proofs of the age of the breed are mentioned to show those who have lately come to admire them that it is not a made-up, composite, or mushroom breed. They are part of Ireland's national economy, and are worthily embodied in the sportsman's toast : ' Irish women, Irish horses, and Irish dogs' (which means, Irish Terriers, Irish Setters, and Irish Spaniels).

One's first acquaintance with the Irish Terrier is apt to be disappointing (except to a really doggy terrier man). It may be because there is no meretricious flash about them; but there is that about them which you learn to like ; they grow upon you. They supply the want so often expressed for a smart-looking dog with something in him. There is that about their rough-and-ready appearance that can only be described as genuine Terrier (or more emphatically Tarrier) character. They are *facile princeps* the sportsman's Terrier, and having never yet been made Fashion's darlings, they retain in all its purity their instinctive love of hard work. Their characters do not suit them for ladies' pets, but render them the best dogs out for the man that loves his gun and quiet sport."

At a later date Mr. Hugh Dalziel, writing of the breed, dis-credits its existence something over thirty years ago, and referring to Mr. Ridgway's letter anent the age and purity of the breed at a very remote date, says : "Surely man never yet 'grounded his faith' on a more slender basis." The patriarch Job, in an old manuscript written in a language older than Irish, refers to the "dogs of his flock"; so when his descendants take to Sheepdog showing, they may "ground their faith" in the antiquity and purity of their Collies by Mr. Ridgway's example, and with as much logical and historical support.

Mr. Dalziel further adds that it is not usual to speak of a date only a score or so of years back as "antiquity," but that is really the date when the origin of the Irish Terrier is lost and found, and by way of winding up says: "When we consider how much we owe to the Irish in dogs, the Wolfhound, the Greyhound, the Spaniel, the Setter, we may readily, and without strain of faith, believe that such a sporting race kept a 'breed of Terriers also,' but to ask us to believe that the show dogs of the present day are purely descended from the Terriers of the 'Long-boat' men is rather too much."

This is quoted to show the difference in opinion that exists as to the real origin of the Irish Terrier.

Probably the show specimens of the present day are not absolutely pure descendants of the Irish Terrier as known in Ireland forty years ago; but there is certainly a big percentage of that blood in their composition, and were proof of this required, it could be forthcoming over and over again. Mr. Dalziel was doubtless actuated by the purest motives in all that he said; but had he dived deeper into the subject, he certainly would have found that the breed did exist in Ireland years and numbers of years prior to its advent on the show-bench in either that country or our own, and might then have deemed it prudent to be less caustic in his remarks, and not quite so hard on a breed that so many have come to admire, and which without flattery may be considered one of the best of present-day Terriers.

The writer holds no brief for Mr. Krehl or any one else, but he must say, in fairness to those who have expressed opinions adverse to those of Mr. Hugh Dalziel, that he has at some considerable trouble made personal inquiries in almost every part of the land of the shamrock, from Londonderry in the north to Limerick and Waterford in the south, and from Dublin in the east to Galway in the west, and has it on unimpeachable authority that the breed has been well known and kept in various parts of Ireland as long as the oldest living man can remember. A personal friend of the writer in County Wicklow, whose veracity may be vouched for, told him many years ago that he had kept the breed for upwards of thirty years. And this is typical of many assurances from men whose statements are beyond suspicion, which might reasonably be accepted as sufficient proof that the Irish Terrier is not quite of the mushroom-like growth that Mr. Dalziel would have us believe.

Although good specimens were known in Ireland long before dog shows were in existence, it must not be taken for granted that collectively they were of the high class we are so accustomed to see now. A change has naturally come about with this, as with many other breeds that have been carefully bred for ex. hibition for thirty years. They were rather a scratch lot, or perhaps more correctly described as bad specimens of the present type. They were dogs that in many cases were light in colour, and had coats sufficiently long to kink or curl, that were woolly in texture, while they varied in weight from between 16lb. to 40lb. This can readily be understood when it is remembered that there were no shows or other inducements to improve the breed. So long as Pat would catch a rabbit, retrieve a wounded bird, watch the house at night, and give any intruding tyke (be he little or big) a rough ten minutes if required, he answered all practical purposes for his owner.

Irish Terriers were first exhibited at Dublin in 1873, and the breed's subsequent successful career is almost wholly due to the zeal and energy of the pioneers, Messrs. Morton, Erwin, Ridgway, Montgomery, Jamison, Corbie Smith, Dr. Marks, Dr. Carey (the present Hon. Sec. of the Irish Terrier Club), Mr. G. R. Krehl, Mr. W. Graham, and a few others. These gentlemen had the uphill part of the business to do in bringing the breed to the front. Many were the ideas and opinions at that date as to what was a typical Irish Terrier. Consequently at shows where the breed was represented, one saw a very mixed lot. And the judging, too, was most erratic. First one dog would get the premier award, then another, and eventually both were headed by a specimen that had no right to be in the class. This naturally caused the greatest dissatisfaction to exhibitors, and finally in 1879 resulted in a club being formed, and a description of the breed drawn up. Later on specialist judges were appointed, and this did wonders in healing the breach brought about by previous bad judging, and cemented the bonds of friendship between the English and the Irish contingents.

From that time the popularity of the breed was assured, and was not long in reaching its zenith. Having a standard to breed to, the merest novice had a guide, and a direct incentive to try his luck, and at the present time the chance of a really good dog at any show being left in the cold is reduced to a minimum. The Irish Terrier has not had the benefit of a pretty face and genteel appearance to help him, but has won his way to the fore on sterling merit.

It is pleasing to record that our beloved King Edward VII., who, as every one knows, is one of the finest sportsmen in the world, has added an Irish Terrier to his famous kennels. This augurs well for the breed, and as an Englishman is nothing if not fashionable and patriotic, we may in the near future reasonably expect to find many more of his Majesty's loyal subjects going in for a " Dare-devil."

Mr. Vero Shaw in his book says that at Belfast, in June, 1878, Mr. Despard's Tanner (afterwards first, Birmingham), took first, second going to old Sport, and third to Mr. W. Graham's Sporter. In bitches Kate was first and Moya Doolan second. At Newtownards, in September the same year, the opinions of experts were encouraging. The eye had not the same chance of being offended at shows as in former years, the majority of the weeds having disappeared. Mr. Graham won, with Sporter, the champion cup for best dog or bitch exhibited. In open dogs Parnell and Tanner II. were first and second respectively. In the bitches Moya Doolan beat Colleen Dhas.

At Birmingham, in December, 1878, Tanner was first and Fly second. Fly had no right to her place, and it was characteristic of the judging that Spuds was quite passed over.

In December, 1878, at the Alexandra Palace, Fly (the second-prize winner at Birmingham) was first, and Spuds second, Paddy II. commended, and Moya Doolan not noticed. This erratic judging caused the dissatisfaction already alluded to, and at the Irish Kennel Club Show in April, 1879, at Dublin, Spuds and Moya Doolan were first and second in champion class. Tanner II. and Paddy II. were respectively first and second in open dogs; and Sting, still a puppy, made her first appearance, and won in open bitches, beating Rags and Kathleen. Gaelic was very highly commended, this being his first appearance. At the Alexandra Palace in July, 1879, Gaelic was put over Sporter and Erin, and a new bitch over Moya Doolan.

It was about this time that Mr. G. R. Krehl put his heart and soul into the Fancy, and this gentleman can honestly claim to have been instrumental in starting the breed in this country. By his purchase of Belle, Splinter, Sporter, Pagan II., and other good dogs, he founded a famous kennel, and a glance at the pedigree of many of the best dogs of the present day will reveal the fact that they contain not a little of the blood of his famous dogs. In the writer's humble opinion Pagan II. was a little too much of the horse-chestnut colour, but in every other respect he was absolutely the best Irishman he had seen up to that time, and he always regretted not using him to his bitch Grovelands Moya, to be referred to later on as having killed a hedgehog smothered with cayenne. This was a cropped bitch, a trifle light in colour, but a rare sort, and was one of a brace purchased in County Wicklow by Mr. Wickens, of Hurst, for £70. This was the time when she was second to Pagan at the Henley Show, and when Mr. Barnett's Bogie Rattler was a puppy, and exhibited for the first time.

Mr. Barnett and his famous dogs are too well known to need mentioning here, except to say that he has been one of the most successful breeders, exhibitors, and judges in England for nearly twenty years. The writer always thought Mr. Barnett's Bachelor was lucky to become a champion, as there was not enough daylight under his body. The writer does like to see an Irish Terrier up on his legs, but not stilty, and, if he is not mistaken, he has seen far more typical Irish Terriers in Mr. Barnett's kennels than Champion Bachelor.

At the Crystal Palace, 1884, Mr. Graham won first in open dogs with his home-bred Garryford (14,578), by Garryowen ex Peggy by Killiney Boy ex Champion Erin ; Messrs. Carey's Mogul (13,844) was second, and Carrick third. Mr. Graham also took first in bitches with Gaily (13,309), bred by Mr. Gourley, Mr. Greaves's Glory (13,558) being second, a bitch that had previously won a first at Strabane and champion prize at Portadown, and also got first in the champion class at the Crystal Palace the following year.

It was at the Kennel Club Show at the Crystal Palace, January, 1884, that the quartet Playboy, Poppy, Champion Pagan II., and Champion Kitty met in the champion class. The first-named three were litter brothers and sister—truly a remarkable litter. Poppy won, and also accounted for the silver medal for the best Irish Terrier in the show, leaving Playboy to do battle later, which he did by winning first Belfast, first and cup Alexandra Palace, first Dublin, first Darlington, first challenge class at the Royal Aquarium Show 1886—in fact, beat about everything he met.

A nice bitch out this year was Mr. Greaves's Extreme Carelessness by Sport ex Vic, and beyond being a little smutty in colour she was hard to beat. She won first in the Challenge Class at the Kennel Club Show at the Crystal Palace in January, 1887, as well as first at the Ranelagh Club grounds later, beating Champion Poppy and Bumptious Biddy. The B's were busy this year. The names of all Mr. Barnett's dogs, it will be noticed, commence with the letter B, and now we find Mr. Graham following suit with the prefix " Breda," and Mr. Backhouse with the prefix " Bumptious."

At the Kennel Club Show at the Crystal Palace, January, 1887, Mr. Barnett's Champion Bachelor won first in the challenge class for dogs, the silver medal for the best uncropped dog, and the special for the best uncropped dog or bitch. He was similarly successful at the Kennel Club Show in February, 1888, winning silver medal for the best Irish Terrier in the show. This dog did a lot at stud, and altogether must have been profitable to his owner. He was by Bogie Rattler ex Biddy III., his grandsire being Playboy and granddam Fury, a bitch that, the writer believes, Mr. Krehl purchased from Mr. Despard. Bogie Rattler and Biddy III. were purchased by Mr. Barnett from Mr. Krehl as puppies. It falls to the lot of only a very few breeders to be as fortunate as Mr. Barnett in breeding a champion at the first attempt.

Mr. Graham again came to the front in 1889 by breeding one of the best in Breda Mixer by Irish Ambassador ex Breda Vixen, winning prizes galore and soon becoming a champion. This dog did a lot of good to the breed at stud, siring many winners, including the invincible Champion Bolton Woods Mixer, out of Saskatchewan, the property of Mr. G. W. Cragg. Bolton Woods Mixer has probably sired more winners and won more prizes for his present owner, Mr. Sam Wilson, than any Irish Terrier that ever lived, and such a little gold-mine must this Terrier have been that he has been facetiously called by some "Daily Bread."

Mr. Graham sold Breda Mixer to Mr. A. E. Clear, who passed him on to the Rev. D. F. Wright, his present owner. The old dog, in addition to being very game, was a splendid companion, and quite one of the rev. gentleman's family.

Bolton Woods Mixer was born February 12th, 1895, which is getting down to a comparatively recent date, and space will not permit of many other good dogs living being mentioned, and were it otherwise no practical good would accrue, as all Irish Terriers of note whelped subsequent to date named are too well known to be referred to here. The writer may, however, be pardoned for harking back to name that nice brace of Terriers, the property of Mrs. Butcher, Bawnboy and Ted Malone, the former by Champion Brickbat ex Lotion and the latter by Champion Daniel II. ex Lotion, both bred by that lady, who, with her dog Still Another, won the first Breeders' Cup outright and many other valuable prizes.

Mr. F. Wheatley's bitch Lewisham Banshee, also a daughter of Daniel II., well merited Mr. L. C. P. Astley's description of her—"A very sweet bitch, hard in coat, and good in body, legs, and feet"; also her many firsts under Messrs. Raper, Gresham, etc. She was a little dark in ear, but the best-coated bitch the writer ever saw.

Mr. F. Butler's Odiham Bridget, a '92 bitch by Odiham Pat ex Gyp, was a winner of several firsts and specials under Dr. Carey, and but for an accident to her thigh would have been a hard nut to crack.

Constitutionally, the Irish Terrier is as hard as a pebble from puppyhood to old age, which renders him one of the easiest to breed. Nothing seems to trouble him so long as there is a bone in the cupboard, and he is as happy on a straw bed in a kennel as reposing on a down cushion in a drawing-room, and a more reliable dog with children cannot be found. As a companion he is hard to beat—a genial, rollicking, good-natured chap, who does not mind waiting outside for an hour or two for his master, even if it does rain or snow. The day is never too cold and the drain never too wet or long if there is a quarry at the other end. He is always a faithful "pal," never surly or snappish, and will take any amount of banter from other dogs before cutting up rusty; but if he happens to drop across a quarrelsome tyke that positively will not take no for an answer, you will see him stand as firm as a rock, with every muscle set ready for action, a slight pucker in the top lip showing a rat-trap-like set of ivory white teeth, which is a plain indication that he means business, whilst his bright, intelligent, hazel eyes flash expressive of the popular saying "Let 'em all come," and the gintleman who is bold enough to tread on the tail av his coat will have a warm time, and will not miss the first opportunity of clearing off with a lasting recollection of "Irish hot." He has been truly designated the Bull-terrier of the sister isle, and it is not too much to say he has few equals and no superior in point of pluck, if the English Bull-terrier be excepted.

In the early eighties Mr. Frank Butler, of Irish Terrier fame, and the writer had been out ferreting rats. On returning home an old cropped Irish Terrier bitch belonging to the writer had killed a hedgehog, which it was subsequently ascertained had been nicely dusted with cayenne, tied up in an old handkerchief, and put on a seat as a "plant" to win ten shillings from the landlord of the inn at which we called, who had a Bull- and Fox-terrier that he said would kill hedgehogs. The owner of the hedgehog said, "I'll give 'e a suverin for the Tarrier, mister," which, needless to say, was not accepted.

Without a good dog as guard, you may have all your locks, bolts, and bars to keep Bill Sykes out of your house should you leave it unattended, and then he will manage to pay you a visit. If you will only leave Paddy at home in charge, with access to every room, you need have little fear that your temporary absence from the house means losing your plate or any other valuables, for the wily Irishman is like the proverbial weasel, never asleep, and his keen nose and quick ear will not fail to detect a strange footstep, even if the would-be visitor is wearing the regulation silent shoes. And his angry bark will be quite enough to keep the intruder on the other side of the door. Nothing upsets the calculations of these gentry so much as a sharp Terrier. One might also feel perfectly safe on a lonely walk, night or day, with Pat as a companion. A well-trained Terrier will keep close to heel at night, and when strange footsteps are approaching you will hear him give vent to a suppressed growl, and if occasion arose you may rely on his cleaning his teeth on your adversary's trousers and pinching his calf in a way that would be anything but pleasant.

Only recently an Irish Terrier belonging to a labouring man showed the writer a very nice set of teeth through his inadvertently going too near his master's dinner-basket and an old overcoat he was guarding with a zeal it was a treat to see.

A true "Dare-devil" is obviously a workman, and as a sportsman he can give any other Terrier a start and a beating. He takes to all kinds of sport as naturally as possible, and it only requires two or three lessons with an adult dog when ferreting for a puppy to understand the game and kill rats as fast as you please. The wiry jacket, hardy constitution, indomitable pluck, and fine stamina, enable an Irish Terrier to work almost any other dog to a standstill, and, what is more, when he sees the gun or the ferret-box the next morning, he is ready and eager for the second edition.

The writer once visited a farm by invitation for an hour's sport killing rats. A friend was having a barley rick threshed, and when the bottom, or bedding, was reached the rats tumbled out thick and fast, and it was a pretty sight to see a brace of Irish Terriers and an old Sheepdog literally slaughter them. One of the Terriers poked his head into the short straw and brushwood upon which the rick had stood, and seemed to kill the rats two at a time. The trio were not long in accounting for 137. An Irish Terrier has such a punishing jaw, and puts so much dash into killing rats, that one sometimes thinks that they are out of place, and that such sport should be relegated to smaller breeds, for he not only kills them but smashes them with the same apparent ease as one could smash eggs with a mallet.

Without question, rabbiting is the kind of sport that the Irish Terrier excels at—the right dog in the right place, so to speak. A model Irish Terrier is a miniature Irish Wolfhound with a yellow-red coat, and consequently, being built on these racy lines, he is by nature specially adapted for rabbiting in every way.

When ferreting a burrow, a well-trained Irish Terrier will sit on the top, and he seems to know instinctively from which hole the rabbit is likely to come, and if the man with the gun fails to grass his bunny, the Irishman, at a given signal, is after him like a shot from a gun, and if the rabbit has no cover inside of two hundred yards, you may count him in your bag. The writer has repeatedly seen a Terrier of this breed catch rabbits in this distance on their own ground, and it is generally believed that a rabbit when he gets out of his form runs as fast as a hare for the first two hundred yards, and except the Bedlington Terrier no other breed of Terrier can equal the Irish Terrier for speed.

It is very regrettable that this good quality should be the reason for the dog being used for rabbit-coursing, a pastime much in vogue. No true sportsman would, however, care to be seen at one of these exhibitions, which are as cruel as they are disgusting. A rabbit is probably the most meek-hearted of any wild animal, and so timid and frightened is it when turned down in a strange place after spending a night in a sack or a box, or perhaps sent some miles by train, that he reminds one of a frog when he sees a snake after him. A Terrier weighing 14lb. can catch a turned-down rabbit with ease ; but let that same dog turn one up from his natural lair, and he simply would not see which way the rabbit went.

The Irish Terrier, too, has an excellent nose, and it is seldom indeed that he makes a mistake. If he stands to a hole, you may be sure there is a rabbit there. He will, too, mark the exact spot where a ferret is laid up with a rabbit. With a knowing turn of the head, first one side, then another, to try and catch the least sound, he will raise himself and pounce down on his fore feet, as if to say, "Here they are!" and after perhaps half an hour's hard work with a spade, you will find that Pat has told the truth. The Irish Terrier is very fond of the water, and will work a sedge-bed for duck or moorhen as well as a Spaniel.

A friend of the writer in Hampshire regularly shoots over a brace of Irish Terriers, and it is a treat to see them work—quarter a field like a Setter, hunt hedgerow or gorse, however thick, and retrieve to hand fur or feather as tenderly as a well-broken Retriever. In fact, if well broken, you cannot put them out of place at any kind of sport.

The Irish Terrier is much too long in the legs, and not in any way suitable for going to earth for fox or badger; such sport must be left to smaller breeds—the Fox-terrier, Dandie, and others. But above ground, no matter what the vermin, he can and will give a good account of himself—that is, so far as drawing a badger from a tub is concerned. A better test to try a Terrier's pluck is to turn upside-down a large wooden trough about 10ft. long and having one end knocked out. Let the badger go to the far end, and if you have a Terrier that will fetch him out, no matter to what breed he belongs, you have a gem of the first water. The writer knew a Bull-terrier bitch that would do this; but after having one of her legs broken from the bite of a badger, she went more cautiously to work, and it looked comical to see her tuck her front legs under her body when going to one to avoid punishment.

When a person talks of a Terrier killing a badger, you may be sure that he is talking without knowledge—it's all moonshine. The writer has seen a good deal of badgers, and been to many a badger dig in the Tidworth country with the late Assheton Smith and Lord Broughton's keepers. Jack Fricker the Huntsman, and Billy Brice, First Whip, always put in an appearance, and brought some of the very gamest Fox-terriers that could be found —dogs that would go to earth and stay there till dug out hours after. A captured badger turned down in the open would easily run away with three of these Terriers hanging to him. The punishment that a badger can inflict on a dog when in his natural earth is truly terrible, and the Terrier that can kill one in such has yet to be evolved.

Mr. Erwin, speaking ·of Irish Terriers, says they have the peculiarity of often appearing shy and timid, but their true nature soon flashes out on occasion. Some of the pluckiest I have owned had this peculiarity—Tanner, Sporter, Banshee, Belle, etc. This is certainly characteristic of the breed, and one not infrequently hears from those not thoroughly acquainted with it the remark, Are they shy? As a breed the Irish Terrier is not shy—he is naturally reticent, and to demonstrate this just show one a rat in a cage, and you will see him immediately stiffen, his tail assume a perpendicular position, his eyes flash, and woe-betide the rodent when he emerges from captivity. No, there is nothing shy about the Irish Terrier; only warm his blood to the proper temperature, and fear or timidity is absolutely unknown to him.

Those who have had years of experience with this breed need no teaching, but a few hints on breeding, general management, etc., may be of use to the less initiated. Irish Terriers are so hardy in constitution that no special care is required in breeding, such as one would have to give to Yorkshire Terriers, Black-and-tans, Toy Spaniels, and other tender varieties. Good quarters, plenty of outdoor exercise, and a good wholesome diet of cooked food are the principal requirements to ensure getting healthy stock.

The *modus operandi* of a novice is too frequently to purchase from some unscrupulous person a snipy-faced, weedy little bitch, or a big, ungainly, flaxen-coated specimen of very doubtful blood, that bears no affinity to an Irish Terrier, except perhaps in colour, and then plank down his money for the service of a stud dog of totally different outline and character, in the full expectation that the mating will strike the happy medium in the size and quality of the progeny, simply because the sire is a good dog. This is diametrically opposed to the laws of practical breeding, and only brings sad disappointment to the experimenter, wastes his time and money, and stocks the country with mongrels that should never see the light of day.

Beginners in the Fancy would act much more wisely by going to a breeder of repute, and purchase of him a bitch of pure blood, for as the old axiom says, "Blood will tell." This need not be an expensive deal, for most breeders occasionally have surplus stock of this sex that they are glad to dispose of at a moderate price, when not quite good enough for the show-bench. Next a stud dog should be selected that excels and whose ancestors have excelled in the qualities in which the bitch is deficient, and if the advice of a practical man can be obtained to assist in the selection, so much the better. March is the best month in the year to breed puppies, so that they can have at least six months to grow before the cold weather sets in. Of course they may be bred at other times, but autumn-bred puppies seldom do so well as those bred in the spring. Care should be taken in the early stage of gestation to see that the bitch is thoroughly clear of internal parasites; if this is not done, in all probability they will be transmitted to the young, and a big risk is run of losing the lot. Without doubt parasites in puppies kill at least three times as many as distemper, or any other malady, and experience teaches that it is the chief thing to fear in breeding almost any kind of dog. It cannot therefore be too strongly pointed out that it is absolutely necessary to take Time by the forelock in this respect.

A suitable place should be selected for the bitch a fortnight prior to the eventful day, so that she may thoroughly settle down. It should be a place that is moderately warm and free from damp or draught, and a bed of soft oat straw should be provided. Her diet prior to whelping should consist of a liberal allowance of cooked food such as oatmeal, vegetables, and biscuits soaked in the liquor from boiled sheeps' heads, etc., twice daily, the biggest meal to be given at night.

For two or three days after the birth of the pups the bitch should have soft warm food and a small midday meal. A day or two later this may be supplemented with some finely chopped meat until the puppies are weaned. A little fresh raw meat is beneficial for a bitch that has a nest of hungry youngsters almost continually sucking her, and, for choice, grass-fed sheeps' paunches unwashed, finely cut up. It is easy to digest, and the undigested portions of herbage it contains (of which dogs are very fond) cools the blood and acts as a mild aperient. The puppies should be docked when a week old, and they should be allowed to remain with the dam until they are at least six or seven weeks old, when the bitch usually tires of them somewhat, and they will be best separated, and the puppies put into a kennel by themselves, or else sent out to " walk."

On no account should a growing puppy be tied up. If this is done, crooked legs are inevitable, the elbows stand out, and the dog is practically ruined. Such a deformity would certainly be of no use for exhibition or sale. In the absence of plenty of kennel room and unlimited exercising-ground, the best thing to do with puppies as soon as they begin to eat well is to put them out to " walk "—one here and another there—with people in the country willing to take them for a trifling amount per week. They are usually well looked after, get a varied diet of plain cooked food, plenty of exercise, and stand a far better chance of developing their sense of smell than when shut up in town. When six months old they should begin to get shapely, and be fit to do a little on the show-bench or in the field. There is, however, always more or less risk in exhibiting very young puppies.

There is no fixed rule for preparing an Irish Terrier for show; everything depends upon the individual. Whereas one is always as fit as the proverbial fiddle, another takes a good deal of getting ready, by virtue of having too much coat; others there are who by nature never get enough, and are consequently no good for exhibition. Although coat is not everything, even on the back of an Irish Terrier, it is a big item in the programme of his success or otherwise, and therefore a thing to be carefully studied. He would be a foolish man who would select a pony from a Welsh drove and send him to a show ungroomed and unkempt; and precisely the same remarks apply not only to Irish Terriers, but to any other dog kept for exhibition. Any attempt at clipping or singeing a dog's coat is termed "faking." It is a useless and a foolish practice, and renders the operator liable to be suspended from exhibiting for a year or more, if detected by the judge or by the critical public.

Only fair and legitimate dressing is permissible, and as this is not always an easy matter to determine, beginners who aspire to dog showing should attend shows where the particular breed in which they are interested is well represented and carefully note the condition of body and coat of the best dogs. By this means they will learn a good deal from the older hands, and gradually get to know how to complete the toilet. A little practice is worth a lot of theory, and a few lessons by way of ocular demonstration will teach those who are desirous of learning more than any amount of reading upon the subject. In fact, it is practically impossible to teach any one from books how to put down an Irish Terrier or, indeed, any other Terrier in first-class form. Experience is the great teacher, and it must be bought.

To select puppies from the nest is by no means the easy matter that a novice might suppose, and so great is the change in colour and general appearance of puppies of this breed that more than once the writer has known a good judge quite at sea with regard to this choice. It is far wiser to leave the selection, if possible, until after the puppies have shed their milk teeth and are approaching six months old; at that time one has a much better chance of forming an opinion as to whether the dog is likely to turn out a good one or otherwise. In the event of having to make a choice from a nest of Irish Terrier puppies at, say, a month or five weeks old, always pick those with small eyes, a good big head, flat skull, plenty of bone, and front legs that have the appearance of being enlarged at the joints. The colour at this age should be as follows : head and legs a nice yellow-red ; the chest, neck, and under-part of the body lighter, almost fawn-colour, and black hair nearly the whole width and the entire length of back from shoulder to tail. This gradually comes out, and puppies of this breed may be expected to present a somewhat ragged appearance until they are six or seven months old, and often do not get a correct colour until a year old. The writer will not readily forget the look of disappointment on the face of a friend who once asked him to have a look at a litter. They were the first he had bred, and were a very level lot, but the breeder had quite made up his mind to find them when only a few days old as perfect in colour as the parents. Some like an Irish Terrier that is deep red in colour, but the majority prefer a nice bright yellow-red, which is the correct one. Good results may be obtained in breeding by occasionally using a dark red, short-coated bitch, providing, of course, the bitch is pure bred, and it is by no means uncommon to get such in a litter.

It is a pleasure to notice at recent shows a big falling off of the red Fox-terrier type, which was so plentiful a few years ago. Nothing has done this variety more harm than the few persistent faddists in breeding these dwarf specimens, and those who have the welfare of the breed at heart will act wisely in giving them a wide berth, as they are uncharacteristic and useless for the purposes for which a good Irish Terrier is justly noted.

It will be observed that the Irish Terrier Club's standard is 24lb. for dogs and 22lb. for bitches ; but it is a well-known fact in Irish Terrier circles that many of the best specimens are considerably in excess of this weight. At the Dublin Show in April, 1900, the Irish members of the Irish Terrier Club unanimously passed a resolution, that no club special should be awarded to any dog exceeding 26lb. or bitch exceeding 24lb., leaving the onus of proving the weight on the objector, the resolution to be subject to the approval and confirmation of the next General Meeting. When the General Meeting subsequently took place at Bristol, the resolution was very wisely rejected by a large majority. It is easy to perceive the bad feeling that might have been caused had this resolution been finally passed. At shows when club specials were given some jealous exhibitors would most certainly have objected to other exhibitors' dogs, and perhaps the grandest living specimen might have been objected to and been compelled to take second place to a very inferior one, simply because he happened to be an ounce or two in excess of 26lb. Besides, weight is not a criterion of size. There are plenty of Terriers that from general appearance one would think heavier than others, but put them on the scales and you will probably find it the other way about.

An eminent authority once said of the breed, when writing of Champion Brickbat (who, by the way, won the Sixty Guineas Challenge Cup twelve times in succession), he could always forgive size for quality ; and this good old dog in his prime probably weighed at least 3lb. in excess of that given by the Irish Terrier Club as the standard weight—namely, 24lb. There is forgiveness for having an Irish Terrier slightly on the big side, providing he is symmetrically built, but there is none for having him small and toyish.

Dr. Carey, too, once said (and we need no better authority) :

" I fear some of our English friends are rather inclined to like a type of Irish Terrier that we Irish do not consider quite the correct one—I mean the small, short-backed dog, with not enough coat, and lacking to a great extent the 'racing build.' I have no hesitation in saying, if this idea is persisted in, we shall have breeders breeding for Fashion, and Fashion's sake, rather than the correct and recognised type."

It was a humane feeling that prompted the Kennel Club to abolish cropping, or, rather, to exclude dogs so mutilated from shows held under its Rules. It was the first nail driven into the coffin of a senseless and cruel practice, now happily relegated to the limbo

Fig. 99.—Mr. C. J. Barnett's Irish Terrier Champion
Breda Muddler.

of forgotten absurdities. Fancy a cropped Terrier poking his head into a rabbit's hole ; he would be certain to get his ears full of sand and dirt. Again, in working gorse, hedgerows, or long grass in wet weather, his poor ears would be sure to get full of water, when ear canker and premature deafness would probably result. The flaps of the ears act as natural protectors for such delicate structures, and in the past the removal of portions of the ears has ruined many a good dog. The cropping was not usually done until the dogs were a year old, and the pain the poor brutes had to endure, until the ears had healed, may be better imagined than described.

Some years ago nearly all the Irish Terriers one saw in Ireland had their ears cut off. They could hardly be described as cropped, as they were not evenly cut to a point to improve appearance, but simply cut straight off about ⅜in. from the head. The writer, of course, is not speaking of exhibition dogs, but those one saw running about the streets in towns in the South of Ireland. It is not so now, for it is quite the exception to see dogs in the Emerald Isle so mutilated.

Since writing this article, the Irish Terrier world is poorer by the death of Mr. William Graham, of Belfast, or, as he was more generally known, Billy Graham, sometimes called "The Irish Ambassador." Billy was small of stature, but mighty in his ideas of Irish Terriers, witty, a rale Irishman, and had nothing to learn about the breed. One of his last good dogs was Champion Breda Muddler (Fig. 99), so named on account of a muddle that was made in his purchase from a ten-pound selling class at the Crystal Palace. The exact price he paid for him the writer cannot remember : it was somewhere about £20, and it was money well invested, as in addition to being a big prize winner himself the dog sired several champions.

The following are the scale of points and description of the true Irish Terrier, as drawn up by the Irish Terrier Club :—

Head.—Long ; skull flat, and rather narrow between ears, getting slightly narrower towards the eye ; free from wrinkles ; stop hardly visible except in profile. The jaw must be strong and muscular, but not too full in the cheek, and of a good punishing length. There should be a slight falling away below the eye, so as not to have a Greyhound appearance. Hair on face of same description as on body, but short (about ⅓in. long), in appearance almost smooth and straight ; a slight beard is the only longish hair (and it is only long in comparison with the rest) that is permissible, and that is characteristic.

Teeth.—Should be strong and level.

Lips.—Not so tight as a Bull-terrier's, but well fitting, showing through the hair their black lining.

Nose.—Must be black.

Eyes.—A dark hazel colour, small, not prominent, and full of life, fire, and intelligence.

Ears.—Small and V-shaped, of moderate thickness, set well on the head, and dropping forward closely to the cheek. The ear must be free of fringe, and the hair thereon shorter and darker in colour than the body.

Neck.—Should be of a fair length and gradually widening towards the shoulders, well carried, and free from throatiness. There is generally a slight sort of frill visible at each side of the neck, running nearly to the corner of the ear.

Shoulders and Chest.—Shoulders must be fine, long, and sloping well into the back ; the chest deep and muscular, but neither full nor wide.

Back and Loin.—Body moderately long ; back should be strong and straight, with no appearance of slackness behind the shoulders ; the loin broad and powerful and slightly arched ; ribs fairly sprung, rather deep than round, and well ribbed back.

Hindquarters.—Should be strong and muscular, the thighs powerful, hocks near the ground, stifles moderately bent.

Stern.—Generally docked ; should be free of fringe or feather, but well covered with rough hair, set on pretty high, carried gaily, but not over the back or curled.

81

Feet and Legs.—Feet should be strong, tolerably round, and moderately small ; toes arched, and neither turned out nor in ; black toe nails most desirable. Legs moderately long, well set from the shoulders, perfectly straight, with plenty of bone and muscle ; the elbows working freely clear of the sides ; pasterns short and straight, hardly noticeable. Both fore and hind legs should be moved straight forward when travelling, the stifles not turned outwards, the legs free from feather, and covered, like the head, with as hard a texture of coat as body, but not so long.

Coat.—Hard and wiry, free from softness or silkiness, not so long as to hide the outlines of the body, particularly in the hindquarters, straight and flat, no shagginess, and free from lock or curl.

Colour.—Should be " whole coloured," the most preferable being bright red, red, wheaten, or yellow red. White sometimes appears on chest and feet ; it is more objectionable on the latter than on the chest, as a speck of white on chest is frequently to be seen in all self-coloured breeds.

Size and Symmetry.—The most desirable weight in show condition is, for a dog 24lb., and for a bitch 22lb. The dog must present an active, lively, lithe, and wiry appearance ; lots of substance, at the same time free from clumsiness, as speed and endurance, as well as power, are very essential. They must be neither " cloddy nor cobby," but should be framed on the " lines of speed," showing a graceful " racing outline."

Temperament.—Dogs that are very game are usually surly or snappish. The Irish Terrier as a breed is an exception, being remarkably good tempered, notably so with mankind, it being admitted, however, that he is perhaps a little too ready to resent interference on the part of other dogs. There is a heedless, reckless pluck about the Irish Terrier which is characteristic, and, coupled with the headlong dash, blind to all consequences, with which he rushes at his adversary, has earned for the breed the proud epithet of " The Dare-devils." When " off duty " they are characterised by a quiet, caress-inviting appearance, and when one sees them endearingly, timidly pushing their heads into their master's hands, it is difficult to realise that on occasions, at the " set on," they can prove they have the courage of a lion, and will fight unto the last breath in their bodies. They develop an extraordinary devotion for their masters, and have been known to track them almost incredible distances.

SCALE OF POINTS

POSITIVE POINTS			NEGATIVE POINTS		
Head, Ears, and Expression	...	20	White Nails, Toes, and Feet, *minus*		10
Legs and Feet	...	. 15	Much White on Chest	... ,,	10
Neck	... ...	... 5	Dark Shadings on Face	... ,,	5
Shoulders and Chest	...	... 10	Mouth Undershot or Cankered	,,	10
Back and Loin	...	... 5	Coat Shaggy, Curly, or Soft	,,	10
Hindquarters and Stern	...	10	Uneven in colour ...	... ,,	5
Coat	... ...	... 15			
Colour	... ...	... 10			
Size and Symmetry	...	... 10			
Total	...	100	·Total	...	50

82

The Irish Terrier

This is unquestionably a very ancient variety of dog, indigenous to the Emerald Isle, in certain features being a modification of the Wolfhound of that country.

Practically, there is no history of the breed, its origin being involved in obscurity.

Ballymena and County Wicklow are said to have been the chief birth-places of these Terriers. Although but a speculative statement at its best, it is a very probable one, and in accordance with what one knows of the history of many other breeds. More recent history of the breed may be said to date from about 1875, marked by their appearance on the show bench in Ireland and the following year in England. They are excellent vermin Terriers, very affectionate to those to whom they become attached, and, as a rule, exceedingly good-tempered. Their dash and pluck has earned for them the *sobriquet* of "Dare-devils," as in the case of the Scottish Terrier—"Die-hards."

These Terriers should have a black nose, strong and level teeth, small hazel-coloured eyes, small V-shaped ears, directed forwards, so as to fall closely to the sides of the head, free from feather, and the hair on them of darker shade than the rest of the body. A Dudley (red) nose will disqualify. The head long, like that of a Fox Terrier, the skull flat, and from the lower jaw there should be rather longer hairs, forming a sort of beard—a characteristic feature of the Dare-devil. A good punishing lower jaw is essential. The head, jaws, teeth, and eyes constitute fifteen per cent. of value in the Irish Terrier Club's scale of points, only equalled by that of the coat.

Coat.—Straight and flat, free from any curl, and of hard or wiry texture.

A soft coat very detrimental, as in the Wire-haired and Scottish Terriers. If the hair of an Irish Terrier is too long, he loses the contour of body, and this ought not to be so.

Colour.—Bright red is much preferred. Some are yellowish-red, others yellow, wheaten and grey.

Brindle will disqualify, and white on feet is a fault, less detrimental, in the judge's eye, when on the chest, but, as in nearly every other breed, Irishmen are better without any white hair.

Neck.—To be of moderate length, carried well up, having a slight frill on either side of it, and ending in strong shoulders, of good shape, with a chest of medium width.

Body.—The Irish Terrier has rather a long body,

IRISH TERRIER BLACKBROOK BANKER.

Barkerend Masterpiece

AIREDALE TERRIER DOG.

due to, in part at least, to the rather narrow—though very muscular—upper part of the thighs, increasing the flank area. In this region the breed is somewhat shallow. Strong loins and the so-called "gay" carriage of tail is requisite. Dock not too short.

Limbs and Feet.—Must be free from feather. Feet small, compact, and black toe nails. Forearms of medium length, straight, with plenty of bone and muscle.

Many Irishmen have very poor fore-limbs, either too long, bent, or weak.

Must be well set up in front, and free movers in both fore and hind-limbs.

Weight.—About 20 lbs., a few pounds more or less being unimportant.

Club.—The Irish Terrier.

Prices.—First-rate puppies can be got at three and four guineas each.

IROQUOIS BENCHER
A consistent winner and good sire. Property of Mr. L. Loring Brooks,
Boston, Mass.

CH. ERIN
From a drawing of the general type of
Ideal illustrations about 1880

CH. PLAYBOY

FULL O' FIGHT
Illustrative of modern ideas as to the Irish terrier in the "tinkering" of
the photo. The old-time ideal is shown by the drawing of Ch. Erin
on this page

CH. SPORT
One of the first Irish terriers shown

CH. BACHELOR

KATHLEEN
The first Irish terrier shown in America, entered in Miscellaneous class,
New York, 1880.

ROYAL BANDMASTER

The Irish Terrier

IT IS little use trying to grope back for any history of the Irish terrier. In 1879, when the breed was being taken hold of and pushed to the front, Mr. Ridgway wrote that there were references to it in old Irish manuscripts, but the only way to make that evidence·tell is to produce or quote from these alleged old manuscripts, and that has never been done. Billy Graham's quizzical explanation of why this most ancient of dogs was not mentioned in the manifest of Noah's ark was that there was no need for him to have inside accommodations, owing to the ease with which he could swim alongside. Another piece of excellent evidence for those who believe in jumping at every straw is the red dog with green head in an Egyptian funeral cortege, painted sundry thousands of years ago.

Dismissing untenable conjecture, we find that from the time the terrier of the North of Ireland became in any way known, he was a dog which, from his being the rangiest of the terrier family of that time and the general resemblance in outline of the best specimens to a rough, coarse greyhound, indicated his descent from the hound dog of Ireland, the Irish wolfhound, brother-in-blood to the Scotch deerhound. The wolfhound, whether short or rough coated, for they seem to have been of both varieties, was red or fawn in colour, and the terrier ran to that colour also, though of course as he was of mongrel breeding there were variations of colour. At the early Irish exhibition of terriers they were, to quote the words of Dr. Carey, the Irish Terrier Club secretary, "of all sorts, sizes and colours." The first really good one was Spuds, shown in 1876. The illustration in Dalziel's book is a good one, and shows what was considered in those days to be the correct form of this terrier. She was cropped, as were most of the Irish terriers of her time, though Mr. Jamison's Sport was not, nor was Mr. Graham's Sporter, afterward Mr. George Krehl's. These terriers were soon followed by Erin, the best terrier of the early days, and while there m a have been a better one since, we can only say that never until we set eyes on Mr. O. W. Donner's American bred Milton Droleen did we see anything that in any way reminded us of the great Erin. We so told Mr. Donner the first time we saw her on the occasion of our judging at Providence, and when she was taken to England Mr. Krehl wrote of her as the "American Erin." Droleen was a cropped bitch and showed the typical head of Erin and the same outline of body, which is that shown in Spuds. We first saw Erin when we ran down to Barrow from Manchester to meet "Billy" Graham, who was going to stop there over Sunday on his way from Belfast to the Palace Show. That was in 1879, and Erin beat all comers at that show, and deservedly. As we propose quoting from an article on the early Irish terriers written by Mr. J. J. Pim, who had a far more thorough acquaintance with her and all the early terriers than we had, as well as of those shown after we left England in 1880, we will not go into particulars regarding Erin. We do not dispute for a moment that Mr. Pim, who knew her so well, is correct in saying that she had a dark red coat, but if we had been asked from recollection to give her colour we should have said red wheaten. In the old days what we now call red wheaten was then called red, and the wheaten was a much lighter shade. Others ran into a sort of grey, resembling the colour of Mrs. Murray Bohlen's Pinscher dog. In size they ran from Spuds and our Banshee down to terriers of the size of Breda Tiny, the typical little terrier imported by Mr. Mitchell Harrison, and from whom came Widow Bedott.

At the head of the old breeders of Irish terriers, as well as exhibitors, Mr. George Jamison of Belfast is entitled to the first rank, and he still has some pretty good ones, though his fancy has turned to trumpeter pigeons, as we found on visiting him a year ago. Mr. Jamison owned Sport, Spuds, and a whole lot of good ones of the early days, and bred many good ones. Still, there is no gainsaying that Mr. William Graham, the great "Billy" known to all dog men interested in Irish terriers, and the original "Irish Ambassador"—so styled from his constant visits to all the important shows in England—was the man above all others who did most for the advancement of the Irish terrier. In addition to dogs of his own he had charge of Mr. J. R. N. Pim's dogs, and all the get of Erin we owe to Graham. After them came his great record of the Bredas, culminating in Breda Mixer and Breda Muddler. Graham liked the dog of medium size, but was shrewd enough to show what would win, and when the judges began to display their preference for the larger dogs and bitches he had that kind to put in front of them. To mark their appreciation of what the late Mr. Graham had done for the breed the Irish Terrier Club members subscribed for a cup, known as the Graham Challenge Cup, which is competed for by all comers at certain prominent selected shows in Ireland and England, and is considered the blue ribbon trophy of the breed. Starting as he did with the foundation stock, from which we have the present day terrier, Graham had an undoubted advantage over the English breeders, who were without intimate knowledge of the characteristics of some of the early and unshown dogs which appear in old pedigrees, and we find in the pedigrees of his latest and best dogs that he practically relied on dogs bred either by himself, or whose parents were of his stock.

Graham was not a stickler for pedigree, but stood for knowledge of what the parents looked like and what their ancestors were. At times he would breed from an inferior-looking dog, such as in the case of Benedict, whose brother Bachelor was the crack dog. One of the valuable photographs we got from Mr. Jamison shows what Benedict looked like, and it would take some persuasion for any person to breed to such a dog. The story was that Graham visited the owner of the two brothers with the real intention of buying Benedict, but only took him at a gift price when his overtures for Bachelor were declined. We have been told by a close friend that such is not the case, and that he only took Benedict because he could not get the other and did not want to go home without doing business.

Something that can easily be learned from these old illustrations is the change of type. The old original standard was framed at the time the breed was started as a show breed, and was drawn up by those who were best qualified to know the correct type. These old dogs we illustrate were considered typical specimens under that standard, but they in no way resemble our winners of two years ago. Garryford and Gaily are good instances of what the cropped Irish terriers looked like, but there is not one of them that shows what has been called the "coffin" muzzle, which began in the Meersbrook Bristles era in wire-haired fox terriers. Selection of this style of foreface could to some extent affect the type, but we are convinced that in many of the English-bred dogs, particularly those of Yorkshire breeding, the Airedale has been introduced. How are we otherwise to account for the heavy ears, placed Airedale style, and the gawky hind legs, together with the tendency to overgrowth? We have never found this in the Irish strains, nor in the kennels of thoroughly reputable Yorkshire breeders of Irish terriers, but among those of shady reputation or when it comes to a dog bred by a man totally unknown, with the probability that the name is only a stop gap. It is very risky breeding from any such dog, or his or her descendants. In our show going, which has extended from the Atlantic to the Pacific and through Canada, we have met with large red dogs, frequently smooth-coated, all possessing the heavy side-placed ears and the comparatively sluggish look of the Airedale, and invariably we have found that they have been bred from dogs of Yorkshire origin.

It was to Yorkshire we owed that monstrosity, the "Taneous" head, the narrow round skull with sunken temples, sometimes with an exaggeration of length of foreface, the narrowness of which was covered up with a wealth of fluffy hair, not Irish at all. None of the old dogs we illustrate show any of this exaggeration of whiskers. "Oh," says the new beginner who has learned Irish terriers thoroughly in a few weeks, "that is the beard, the standard says it has to have a beard; it is the beard." Not at all; the beard is a tuft or two of hair growing on the under jaw, and the old Irish terrier was about as clean muzzled as an Airedale. We do not object to a little bristly growth along the jaws, so long as it is free from lintyness or fluff, for that most assuredly indicates that the body coat is not sound, no matter if it looks so for the time being. Dogs of this kind are seen now and again throughout the year, but have periods of retirement during which the all-the-year-round, sound-coated dog is being shown.

Americans are not so much to blame for getting astray, as they did a year or so ago, on the question of type. Dogs sent from the other side were represented to them as being the correct type. We saw one communication from an importer to the effect that the dog he was then trying to sell was "the new type that is doing all the winning on the other side."

Relying upon the representations regarding these dogs, good prices were paid for them, the purchasers not realising that they had not the correct thing until the next importation of the only genuine, correct type was received, when they realised that "type" meant only the dog that was for sale, and varied as the dogs did.

This could not last for ever, and the importation of a large number of good dogs that were winning on the other side, where also there had been a radical return to something nearer the old type, settled the question, and the day of the dog with the "Taneous" head was at an end. The name

CH. ENDCLIFFE MUDDLE.

BLACKBROOK BANKER

Photo by Rosemont Leeds, Eng.

LEEDS AMBASSADOR

CH. STRAIGHT TIP

CH. BRICKBAT

Considered one of the most typical dogs of his day

SARAH KIDD

One of the best terriers of a few years ago in the Belfast district

93

Taneous came from a dog which had a very narrow, long head, and anything approaching his style of head still goes by his name.

Another change of a desirable nature has been the return to something more like the right thing in the condition of coat on the exhibition dog. The Irish terrier is a rough dog and should look as if he was rough, without it being necessary to rumple up the coat to see if it is any length. We have seen Irish terriers win, and that under judges whose names appear on the list as approved by our Irish Terrier Club, when they had no more coat than that of a smooth fox terrier. That is, however, dying out with the Taneous head and the equally erroneous idea that the Irish terrier should have a long, square muzzle, or what Mr. Fred Breakell of Manchester calls the "coffin" muzzle. What we want to preserve in the Irish terrier is the expression. This is different from that seen in the fox terrier, the Scotch, the Airedale or the bull terrier, just as each of them differ from all others.

At one time our judges went solely for length of head, but that has met with a timely death, and we are really closer to the correct thing in our judging than for some years now. In place of balking at everything but a narrow head and long foreface the same men are now going to the opposite extreme, and we have short, square-headed dogs winning, for no reason than that they have good legs and feet. There is moderation in everything and in our opinion the first thing a judge should look for is the Irish expression, the one thing especially indicative of the breed. If you get that the head is pretty sure to be not far from right. Then comes the racing outline of the breed, which calls for not too much width of chest, though the fox terrier front is equally wrong, the pasterns springing a little. He should show sufficient length of leg to look as if he could extend himself a bit, and to do so the back ribs do not want to be let down as in a cobby dog. A modified greyhound cut-up in the loin, and good length from hip to hock, while a gay carriage of tail assists materially in setting off the "Dare devil."

In the old days we showed our Irish terriers in what would now be called the rough. They were brushed with a dandy brush, and the only thing we learned from Graham in this line was that the hair which was apt to overrun the edge of the foot and make it look large and flat, should be "shingled" off with a poor cutting knife edge, so as not to make jagged cuts. That was done a month or six weeks before an important show. We do not say that even at that date there was not a trimmed or plucked dog; in fact, we know one that was. That was Gaelic, a dog Graham had, and as at that time there was little love between Graham and the club secretary, Dr. Carey, we were surprised to hear that Graham had sold Gaelic to him, for the dog had done quite a bit of winning. Next time we met Billy we asked the reason for the sale. "Well, Gaelic is not the best-coated dog in the world and I'm a busy man. Now the Doctor isn't. He ives away down there at Borris, with hardly a thing to do, and he is in a fair way to go to the bad if his idle hands are not occupied, so out of real friendliness and a desire for his salvation I sold him Gaelic, and—he'll keep him busy." We do not remember the dog being shown much, if at all, after that. Anyway that was the only dog that we ever heard of that was presumably tampered with or prepared. We never used the terrier combs that are a necessity nowadays and tend to tear out the under coat, as well as the old coat that may be removed.

That style of showing we are never likely to return to, but we most certainly are exhibiting our dogs more naturally than was the case a year or two ago, when trimming was carried to an unwarranted extent. We have only seen one case of extreme trimming this season, when the head of a well-known bitch was outrageously barbered. That was bad enough, but we regret to say that for the first time we saw during the present year the pernicious filling of the coat with a preparation of rosin. We saw two dogs so treated, and as we were exhibiting against them we told the persons interested in them to brush them out at once and never let it be done again at any show we attended. This was at once complied with. One of the dogs was owned by an amateur and he expressed surprise that we objected, saying that every person did it. We responded that such was not the case, and only once before had we seen such a thing. It is perhaps a little difficult to say exactly where preparation by trimming ceases to be legitimate. Still, the line of deception as to a dog's demerit is not altogether undistinguishable, and anyway rosin in the coat is fraud, pure and simple. The question is solely that of deception practiced on the judge, or sought to be practiced on that official, and not that of the preparation of the dog in a legitimate way. It is not deception to clean up a dog's feet so that they are of good shape, round and well knuckled up, for that is not deceiving the judge, but to clip, singe, or pluck a naturally woolly headed dog is deception, for with his woolly topknot he would soon be turned out of the ring. That is the vital point of the question of trimming.

As may be surmised from our introductory remarks there is no ancient history of this breed. We go back to about 1870 in the longest extended pedigree that can be made up out of the English stud book, or from any other source that we have knowledge of. Some years ago Mr. O. W. Donner asked us to undertake the extending of the pedigree of a son and daughter of his Milton Droleen, and by Breda Muddler. We did so as far as the stud book data would carry the pedigree and then sent the result across the Atlantic to a friend, who had instructions as to every line of investigation to be followed and who to see or write to. Every person lent the readiest assistance and Messrs. Jamison and Graham pored over the pedigree, adding links here and there from their old recollections, but there was no getting any further back than we had already done in the longest extended lines, and they came to an end with dogs that did not go back to 1870. It was only in the extension of the same dog's pedigree, as it reoccurred, that we reached that link. It is not an old breed so far as pedigree making goes, and they did not always come true to colour in the litters either. Others besides ourselves ended the career of what might have turned out to be pretty good "Welsh terriers" had there been such a breed in existence then, but all black and tans went into the water bucket. Mr. Barnett attributes this colour to Killiney Boy, who he says was out of a black and tan dam, but we drowned black and tans before Killiney Boy was known as a sire.

The good dogs of those days were picked up here and there by good judges, and when it was known that a man would give a good price for a dog he would have dogs offered him from many parts of the country. There was no pedigree behind them, and it was only the judicious mating by such men as Graham, though he was almost an exception in the way of ability in this direction, that laid the foundation for the present good displays of Irish terriers. Belfast was then the headquarters for the breed and it has ever remained so in respect to Ireland, though as may be supposed, there have been and are many other breeders there. In England it was taken hold of by Mr. George R. Krehl, who, upon the advice of Mr. Vero Shaw, then kennel editor of the *Live Stock Journal*, kept the name of the breed before the public by means of discussions and letters contributed by himself and friends till the time was ripe for starting a specialty club. This was done in 1879, and in May of that year Dr. Carey, who is still the secretary of the club, issued his first circular giving the names of twenty-five Irish and twenty-seven English members. Of the entire number we believe we are the only one on the list who is showing Irish terriers at the present time. A good many of the English members were merely friends of Mr. Krehl and never owned one of the breed, but they started the club at any rate and others took their places. One of the important steps early taken by the club was in the direction of natural ears, the credit of which is due Mr. Krehl, who pushed the original movement and made it easy for those who ultimately got the Kennel Club to accede to the request to prohibit cropping after a specified date; a step which eventually led to the prohibition being extended to all breeds.

At that early date there were a good many uncropped dogs. Mr. Jamison's old dog Sport had natural ears, so had Mr. Krehl's Sporter and his Moya Doolan, but these were mainly dogs picked up here and there that had not been bred in kennels where show dogs were raised. The regulars held out for cropping, in the main, Graham being very much against any change as spoiling the look of the dogs. When the rule was passed all had to obey it, and the rule was followed in this country when the Irish Terrier Club of America was organised. In those old days we made a fuss about immaterials, as all novices do. We had it in other breeds and while St. Bernard men thought everything about dew claws we discussed the question of disqualifying dogs with anything but black toe nails, how much white might be permitted on a dog's breast and trivial points of that kind, just as new beginners do to this day. After English exhibitors learned more they went for real terriers and the once burning question of the colour of toe nails was buried, though it still survives in the standard as a relic of the past.

We will now give the "recollections" of Mr. J. J. Pim, which must have appeared originally at the close of 1891, seemingly, for he apparently wrote on dogs shown a few months before. We extract the communication from the *Irish Terrier Review* of July, 1905, which fails to give the original source of publication, though stating that it is republished by Mr. Pim's permission:

IRISH TERRIERS—PAST AND PRESENT

"Having been asked to give 'my recollections' on the above, I have tried to do so from memory, and must ask my readers to excuse any mistakes.

"I always considered the Irish terrier of the North of Ireland the truer breed, as with few exceptions those from the South were neither

Photo by Allison, Belfast

CH. BREDA MUDDLER

Photo by J. Exley, Bradford, Eng.

CH. BREDA MIXER

high enough on the leg nor hard in coat. I am now speaking of those at our first shows in 1874 and 1875.

"The first show in England that made a class for our breed was Brighton, 1876. Mr. Jamison of Belfast, and Mr. Mawdsley of Liverpool, won, the only exhibitors, the former winning both prizes. Glasgow in 1875 was the first Scottish Show to help us. Mr. A. T. Arrol, who had several goodish ones, was probably the first Scottish exhibitor.

"The first good specimens I remember were Mr. George Jamison's Sport (5,761), first Glasgow, 1875, and illustrated in your paper the same year, with drop-ears (several of our present winners' pedigrees go back to him), and Mr. Norton's Fly (3,524), first Newtownards, 1874, dam of several winners in 1875 and 1876. Mr. Smith's Spuds (6,846), cropped, the best we had yet seen, came out at Cork, 1876, and then found her way into Mr. Jamison's kennels; he won with her and another bitch, Banshee (too thick in head), at Brighton, 1876, and 1877 at the Kennel Club, who had also given the breed a class for the first time. I well remember leading Spuds, and telling Colonel Owen, the judge, that I thought she should have beaten Banshee. I then bought her, and she was my first show Irish terrier, and won first at the Kennel Club Show, beating Banshee, and first Bristol, 1877, etc.; she was rather large, but fit to be in it even now. A nice-sized dog, Mr. Graham's Sporter (7,844), drop-ears, was also shown in 1877. Afterwards Mr. Krehl's well-known winner, and just what we want to-day, with good, bright, red, hard coat; it may here be mentioned that Mr. Graham still sticks to small-sized ones; my idea is the happy medium.

"1878. We first saw Dr. Carey's Champion Sting (cropped), a bitch who lasted marvellously; I judged her at Armagh, 1882; her legs and feet were as good as ever, although twelve years old; she was wheaten in colour. Mr. Waterhouse's Killiney Boy, a rare good little cropped one, rather low on the leg; I gave him his first prize at Belfast, 1879; he afterwards proved himself a very valuable sire.

"1879. I think everyone will agree that the mother and star of the breed (Erin, 9,704) was found by Mr. Graham in her hamper before being benched at Dublin Show; she had come from Ballymena, County Antrim; he bought her out at the Alexandra Palace, 1879, winning first and Irish Terrier Club Challenge Cup the first time competed for, which trophy she afterwards won outright for my brother, and was, I think, never beaten. Most of my readers have seen her, but for those who have not I think her worth describing: Beautiful long lean head, cropped, with that game-looking eye and expression peculiar to the breed that we are fast losing; nice neck, with perfectly placed shoulders, good legs and feet, wonderfully perfect body, stern, and hard dark red coat, not heavy in bone or forelegs, which were not low, but forming a perfect symmetry. As she was when I bought her in 1880 she could have beaten any terrier now showing. She— poor Vic!—died last year in my brother J. R. N. Pim's possession. He bought her from me, and became for some years a very successful exhibitor and breeder. Her first and famous litter to Killiney Boy produced the Champions Playboy, Pagan II., and Poppy; also Pretty Lass, etc., the best of their day from 1882 to 1887 (I consider Playboy the best dog we have ever seen); and afterwards Droleen (first Challenge Darlington, 1891), and several other good ones.

"The club was now started (1879) by Dr. Carey, Mr. George Krehl, and others; it still stands as one of the largest and best of to-day, and may it long remain to do good service to the breed! I still think it made a mistake in stopping cropping too quickly, but I hope in a few years to see as good ears on Irish as on fox terriers.

"1883. Mr. Waterhouse had a grand terrier, Peter Bolger (13,548), cropped, who won at the Kennel Club and other shows.

"1884. Mr. Lamb's Gaily, a good bitch with a white chest; Mr. Krehl's Kitty, very nice, with also too much white; Mr. Graves' Phaudry, with his queer expression; and Mr. Waterhouse's Killiney Boxer (16,711), a rare nice terrier, with good drop-ears and perfect front, but hardly an Irish terrier; can a light tan and black coat be the thing? Mr. Graham's Garryford (14,578), a good dog bar his wide chest, and his Gilford (16,058), correct in type, but too large.

"1885. Mr. Barnett's Bachelor was a big winner, a dog a little too much of the fox terrier in build, who has, I am afraid, given us (with his brother Benedict) that dark expression in their progeny; he had many good points, viz., ears, legs, feet and texture of coat; Mr. Backhouse's Buster (16,057), a fair dog of good type; Mr. Kerrigan's Fiddle (first Dublin), a good red bitch, but wanting in character; Mr. Graham's Extreme Carelessness, a grand one, bar her black hairs (Mr. Graves was now buying at big prices); and Mr. Nicholson's Poppy II., a lovely terrier, light of bone— were the pick of this year.

"1886. Another good buyer in Mr. Hoare turned up, who afterwards

CH. HISTORIAN

RED TREX

FISCAL FIGHTER

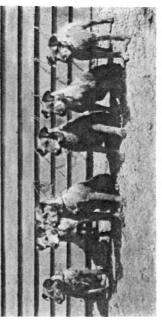

CH. LORTON BELLE, MEADOWS BRIDGET, CH. RED GEM, CH. IN-VERNESS SHAMROCK, LADY HERMIT, ENGLISH NELL

Names are from left to right

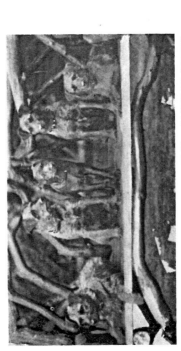

BOGIE RATTLER   BIDDY III   BENEDICT   BACHELOR BRONZE

On the photograph of this group Mr. George Jamison printed the name below each dog. Benedict is a peculiar looking specimen to be the sire he was

won many prizes with Poppy II. and Gaily; Mr. Cotton's Cruisk (first Dublin), a good, large, drop-eared, nice coloured dog; he ought to be still a good sire, as he has already made a name in that line; Mr. Summer's Michael (18,651), famous as the sire of Mr. Wiener's cracks, but not in my opinion a high-class show dog; Mr. Wiener's Norah Tatters (18,089), first Crystal Palace, etc., great quality, but not true in type.

"1887. A very large entry at the best shows, but nothing A1 came out. Mr. Summer's B.A. (21,567), good head (cropped) and colour, but I think the kennel owned a far better in Pedlar (brother to Playboy), one of the best I ever saw, but when I was at Liverpool he was getting old and broad in skull; if he is still alive he ought to be the best stud dog about; Mr. Wiener's Ballyhooley (23,646), a great winner, but although good in body, coat, legs and feet, I think him a very lucky dog; Mr. Graham's Breda Rattle (23,652), wonderfully good legs and feet, very hard in coat, but never a good sort; Mr. Backhouse's Bumptious Biddy (23,686), a good type, a bit short in muzzle, but the best of this year.

"1888. Mr. Wiener made this year to be remembered by the bringing out of the brothers Brickbat and Bencher; the latter is perhaps on the large side, but a grand-headed, typical terrier, and ought to be a good sire for small-sized, lightly coated bitches; Champion Brickbat, when he came out, was a bit weak in face, but he has wonderfully improved, and is to-day the best living. Mr. Graves brought old Playboy again to the front, after retiring for a time; he improved with age; Mr. Charley's Mars (25,938), by Benedict, a grand terrier but for his large eyes and dark expression; Mr. McRae's Irish Ambassador (25,932), a good dog as a sire, and the right type. I had the honour of judging the largest entry the Kennel Club have ever had (at Olympia), and Dr. Carey, at Liverpool, the largest entry at any show up to this date.

"1889. Messrs. Carey came to the fore with a good dog in Pilgrim (28,110), drop-ears, good colour, rare bone, legs and feet; he is now the property of the Earl of Shannon, who paid a big price for him; Mr. Taylor's Breadenhill (28,087), cropped, a dog with one of the very best heads we have ever seen; he has good bone, but few other good points; he is a favourite with some; Mr. Barnett's Bouquet (28,130), drop-ears, a grand bitch, spoiled rather by that dark expression I do not like; Mr. Norton's Miss Peggotty (28,157), a lovely large-sized bitch, with a bull terrier sort of head; Mr. Charley's Dunmurry (28,143), a very typical terrier, with one fault—weak ankles.

"1890. This year we had very strong classes, and a very level lot. Mr. Breakell's Bonnet (30,308), a very good one, just a little broad in skull, and too much muscle outside her front, perfect legs and feet, colour, coat, and type; Mr. Graham's Breda Mixer (30,269), one of the best puppies I ever saw; he combines character and quality, with good head and nice front; he may some day beat the lot; he is now the property of the plucky Mr. Mayall. Mr. Backhouse's Bumptious Blue Stocking (30,013), a good typical bitch, rare head and expression; it was well she was not put in bucket in her early youth, as she was sold to Mr. Krehl for £100, I am told, and he again sold her to the Earl of Shannon. Mr. Backhouse's Bumptious Blazer (cropped when stolen), a very good little dog; I like him very much when fit, but for his muzzle, which is too weak; he brought in another £100 for his lucky breeder; Mr. Wiener's Merle Grady (30,292), a rare terrier, just the size and type; he is a bit loose in elbows; Mr. Barnett's Beautiful Star (30,262), a wonderfully well-made terrier, wrong in type and expression; Mr. Krehl's Dan'l II. (30,277), a good little sort, not straight; Belfast Show had the record entry; Mr. Vicary the judge.

"1891. The Earl of Shannon is buying right and left, and we all wish him good luck; but he has two very good kennels to beat—Messrs. Wiener's and Graham's. Mr. S. Pratt's Boddy (first Darlington), a very good puppy, with nice drop-ears, good bone, front, and body, matured-looking for her age when we judged her in July, and too profuse in coat. I only hope she will last and improve; a real good stamp. Mr. Wiener's Bucket, a nice youngster, with bad ears, and a little wanting in expression, but one like improving much, and I expect to see her a high-class bitch, perfect body, front, and coat; Mr. Graham's Breda Ida, a very grand bitch, and very nearly the best going; her ears and eyes might be smaller; bar this she is good everywhere; Mr. Boyle's Churchtown Chippie (first Armagh), a good typical bitch, a rare mover, and I think will grow into a champion; she is now the property of Mr. Graham, who paid a goodish price for her. Belfast again held the record for the largest entry I believe ever obtained; Mr. Barnett judged.

"I must end now, and ask you to pardon the length of my letter. I have only mentioned the best specimens I could recollect, and I am sure I have missed many I ought to have written of."

In this same issue of the *Irish Terrier Review* the editor, Mr. T. R. Ramsey, has this to say under the head of "Progress":

"Have we, as many say, lost the type, character, and expression that distinguished the breed ? That is to say, have we now produced a terrier without the keen, varminty and (in profile) sinister appearance and racy outline that we associate with an Irishman ? No, I don't think we have. Put one of the best terriers we have beside a photo of Brickbat or Ted Malone, and see what is the difference. It is not a difference in type, character, or expression; it is this, and this only—Brickbat lacked ears and face (we would call him bitchy to-day) and Ted Malone lacked face (resembling his sire) in comparison with our present best. The varmintyness is still there, but the absence of the 'crop' detracts from it. If any croaking is required, it appears to be that we must keep our eyes on the coats, and beware of insufficiently bent stifles and hocks that are not low enough—a prevalent fault. No doubt fresh faults crop up (unless it be that old faults become more noticeable), but they are quickly observed and wonderfully quickly eradicated. Think how very prevalent the exaggerated and soft whisker was a few years since, and see how comparatively rare it is to-day; likewise the contracted skull. Both are practically dead with the disappearance from the ring of the 'pioneers' of these faults, whose other many excellencies caused the faults to be overlooked. The great difficulty now is to find a first-class and well-bred stud terrier who is not inbred to one particular strain. Undoubtedly this strain has done wonders for the breed, but one can have too much inbreeding, and Irish terriers are bound soon to 'progress backwards' unless a good and well-bred outcross to remedy this state of things be quickly found and freely bred to. There is another thing most of us do not give sufficient attention to, and that is regularly using our terriers to some form of sport. Nothing gives a terrier life and character, hardness and self-reliance to such an extent as hunting, whether it be rats, rabbits, or cats."

To that we reply as follows: The Irish terrier of to-day is not what the old ones were like and what the standard was made for, more particularly in outline and in foreface, together with expression. We do not mean to say that there is not a single terrier that shows any one of the characteristics named, but that they are not so typical of the breed. Another thing is that we are getting the Irish terriers too large, and we would like to see our Irish Terrier Club adopt a rule to the effect that no club prize could be won by any terrier over a specified weight; just as the Spaniel Club restricts cockers to eighteen pounds and under twenty-four pounds. The

Irish Terrier Club of England and that of this country have the same standard description, and the weight given "as most desirable" is twenty-four pounds for dogs and twenty-two for bitches. We think it would be almost impossible to get a first-class show dog of the present day under twenty-four pounds, and that many of them weigh from twenty-six to twenty-seven pounds. We have made the same mistake the fox terrier men did some years ago and gone in for dogs that are over size. We recently placed a bitch that weighed close to twenty-two pounds over quite a number of terriers that had been winning at various shows, and some of the ring side critics wanted to know why we placed such a little thing in first place. When told that she was the only terrier in the whole of the classes that was within two pounds of the club standard weight they could not believe it possible and wanted to know what the standard weight was. We will admit that many of the old-time terriers were also over the suggested weight. Spuds most certainly was and so was Banshee, they weighing twenty-six or twenty-seven pounds. Erin was nearer the right thing than the most of those shown in her time.

Next to present day size the great difference is in foreface. Mr. Ramsay says we would now call the old dogs "bitchy" in face. That is because the Englishmen have gone in for the wrong sort of forefaces in their dogs, beginning with the days when Meersbrook Bristles and his type swept the judges off their feet and whiskers and an exaggerated face were called for in other varieties of terriers besides the wire-haired fox. There was no loss of "varminty" expression when cropping was stopped, until the sleepy, tired look came in with the "Taneous" head and the fluffy foreface. Our exhibitors have had opportunities of seeing Borthwick Lass, formerly the English champion Winsome Lass, also Borthwick Rascal, formerly Ulidia Rascal. The latter, if cropping made the difference, would be out of it entirely, for his fault is largish ears, yet these two terriers are the two that would probably be picked as showing the Irish lookout, better than any we now have. Neither is in any way exaggerated in foreface, in fact Lass is quite medium in that regard, and she is more typical than Rascal. The little Raynham Olivette is another of the same kind. Right size, racing outline and keen Irish expression.

Mr. Ramsay is unfortunate in picking the photograph of Brickbat as representative of the old type. We have seen that photograph, and while Brickbat may have been a good dog his photograph does not show that he was anything remarkable, and to take him as a type of the days when the standard was framed is certainly erroneous. We cover the old times more fully than has ever been done with the many photographs we reproduce of old dogs, celebrities in their days. For most of which we have to express our indebtedness to Mr. George Jamison. The picture of Erin which is from a drawing made when she was at her best is given not as actualy representing her so much as representing what was to the eyes of Irish terrier men of that time the type of dog they wanted—in other words their ideal. Compare this with the tampered photo of Full o' Fight and some others, "improved" to suit the modern ideas of what an Irish terrier should be in head. Perhaps we ought hardly to say modern as applying to to-day, for we believe there is a disposition to let the "coffin" foreface follow the whiskers and Taneous head into oblivion.

With regard to Mr. Ramsay's remarks as to too much inbreeding to Breda Mixer, through Muddler and Bolton Woods Mixer, where is he going to get the out-cross? What dog is there that has not Bolton Woods Mixer blood in his veins, or Breda Muddler's? But that is nothing to worry about, for we are getting away from them and are already finding them as far back as the third and fourth remove in the pedigrees of the youngsters of to-day. It has been good blood and physically there has been no deterioration, otherwise we would not now be complaining of our dogs getting too large.

In another portion of the same article Mr. Ramsay says:

"Is it true that we have lost the old Irish terrier and replaced him with something different? Well, in a sense it is so. Undoubtedly, we have a different terrier to-day. It would speak badly for the success of our attempts at breeding up to an ideal standard if we remained where we were —all improvement must entail differences between the dog of to-day and his forebear. But I don't for a moment think that the difference is retrogressive; on the contrary, it is progressive; we are much nearer our Club standard than ever we were."

Mr. Ramsay is best answered by the photographs. If the drawing of Erin, and we have several others of that period drawn on similar lines, and the other photographs represent the type of dog that the framers knew and described in the club standard, how can the head of dogs fashioned on the Full o' Fight model be nearer the standard. Such an alteration as that is not getting nearer the standard, for the standard was never made for such a dog and if one of that kind had been led into the ring in the days of Erin and Sporter, he would have got the gate as a monstrosity. It must be understood that the Full o' Fight photograph is not the dog as he actually was, for it is cut out below the jaw, trimmed down the legs, along the back and down the quarters, and we only use it to show the supposed typical dog of three years ago as compared with the supposed typical dog when the standard was framed, as shown in the drawings of the Erin type. Another thing not to be overlooked in connection with the old photographs we reproduce is that they were taken when animal photography was in its infancy, instantaneous work was then unknown, and it is doubtful if a single photographer in England or Ireland knew the first principles of posing a dog.

It is not necessary to go into details regarding the growth of the Irish terrier in England, so we will condense matters by saying that Breda Mixer, the puppy mentioned by Mr. Pim as coming out in 1890 and as likely "some day to beat the lot," fulfilled his estimate. Mixer did beat all comers, was chosen to represent the typical Irish terrier when the Irish Terrier Club wanted a sketch of the correct type, and proved himself the great stud dog of the breed. His two sons, Bolton Woods Mixer and Breda Muddler, are still living, and Muddler is not yet past his days of usefulness as a sire, even at his advanced age.

What descendants they have left from which their successors are to be produced is very uncertain, for at present there is no predominating sire in England. Bolton Woods Mixer's best show son was undoubtedly Straight Tip, now in this country, but though he was as much used at stud as was his sire, his get did not cut such a swathe as did the Bolton Woods Mixer's in the high day of their successes. It is likely that but for the government prohibition against the shipping of dogs from Ireland to England, the merits of Champion Colin would have received proper recognition. It was to countermine the government order that clever Mr. Graham at once shipped Breda Muddler to England, nearly all of his stud patronage coming from there. With regard to Colin we recall that when the late Mr. Rodman, our Irish Terrier Club secretary, returned from a trip to England and Ireland he told us that he considered Colin the best dog he had seen. When we visited Ireland in 1904 we saw so many good dogs by Colin that, bearing in mind Mr. Rodman's report, we specially visited this dog and although he had not the freshness of youth we do not know of a dog that impressed us more than he did, and but for the positive statement of his owner that

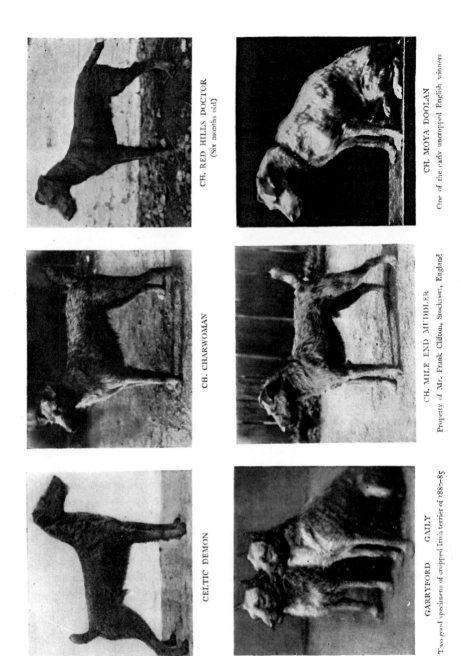

CH. RED HILLS DOCTOR
(Six months old)

CH. MOYA DOOLAN
One of the early uncropped English winners

CH. CHARWOMAN

CH. MILE END MUDDLER
Property of Mr. Frank Clifton, Stockport, England

CELTIC DEMON

GARRYFORD   GAILY
Two good specimens of cropped Irish terrier of 1885-85

money could not induce him to part with the dog we would have made every effort to buy him. He was thoroughly Irish in type, well-built and eminently sound in coat. His line is as much of an outcross as one can get from Bolton Woods Mixer and Breda Muddler at the present time and get a winning strain, for he is three removes from Muddler, reaching him through his sire's dam, that excellent bitch, Champion Blue Nettle. Colin's dam is a daughter of Bolton Woods Mixer, but her dam and also the line of Colin's grandsire are outcrosses. Mile End Muddler is another good dog of the Breda Muddler line, but he does not seem to have been at all phenomenally successful as a sire, in fact there has not been a dog in England since Bolton Woods Mixer's day that has filled his place. We note, however, that Mr. Jowett's Crow Gill Mike seems to be making himself conspicuous.

It is now time to turn attention to the Irish terrier in America, the history beginning with the advent of Kathleen, the bitch we brought over in 1880 and showed in the miscellaneous class at New York that year. Kathleen came from the middle counties of Ireland, and her pedigree did not extend beyond her sire and dam. She had won a third at Dublin before we bought her from Mr. Graham, and for us she won two firsts and a second. She was bred to Mr. Krehl's Sporter, and when lying off Staten Island she gave birth to the first Irish terrier puppies born in this country, one of which won a second at New York in 1881 and when sent to England with his dam a few months later had his name changed and won a prize or two there. Dr. J. S. Niven, of London, Ont., was the next to import a few of the breed, and his Norah and Aileen were winners in their day. Mr. Lawrence Timpson had one or two during the eighties, including the dog Garryowen, by Paddy II. out of Erin, but there was nothing here of any account to produce good results from this dog. Mr. J. Coleman Drayton also imported Spuds when she was eight years old and showed her so fat that she had not the slightest resemblance to the flyer we had seen five or six years before.

Mr. Mitchell Harrison, who was king-pin among collie exhibitors, bought, when in Ireland in 1887, a brace of Mr. Graham's terriers, a fairly good dog named Breda Jim, and a nice quality, rather small bitch named Breda Tiney. Mr. Charles Thompson, also of Philadelphia, at the same time got the bitch Geesela and had her bred to Benedict before bringing her home with him. From this line came the various Geeselas that have appeared at Philadelphia shows. Breda Tiney won at New York in 1888, but Breda Jim was beaten by another Graham dog named Greymount, a son of Gilford. Breda Tiney won at all the leading shows in 1889 and took first in the challenge class at New York in 1890. Mr. Harrison had by this time got a few more of the breed and his Roslyn Dennis and Roslyn Eileen each took a second at New York in 1890, while their son, Roslyn the Mickey, which had been sold to Mr. E. Wetmore, was first in the open dog class.

It was at this show that Mr. Walter Comstock showed Breda Florence, a beautiful bitch of Mr. George Jamison's breeding, but sold by him to Mr. Cinnamond, who named her Red Isis and showed her at Glasgow where she was claimed by Graham, who renamed her, showed her successfully, and then sold her to Mr. Comstock.

Before Mr. Comstock got her she had been bred to Bachelor and one of her litter was the bitch called Iris, sometimes Breda Iris and so registered in England, also Red Iris, and she is a litter sister to Red Inez. This bitch Breda Iris, as she was then, was bred to Graham's Breda Mixer, and from this mating came Breda Muddler. Mr. Jamison, as late as 1900, wrote us that Breda Florence was "the best bitch we ever had of the breed." It was Mr. Comstock's misfortune to lose her by death before she had been here over a year.

With the year 1891 Irish terriers evidently got a grip hold, for thirteen dogs and seventeen bitches were entered in the two open classes at New York that year, when Breda Tiney again did duty by herself in the challenge class. First in dogs came Breda Bill, a full brother to Breda Star, the sire of the dam of Breda Mixer and many others. Second to this dog came Mr. Comstock's Mars, a brother to Sauce, who was the dam of the dam of Breda Mixer. This shows that at that time we had some good material in this country, but unfortunately did not make the use of it that we might. Mr. Comstock had Dunmurry to take the place of Breda Florence at the head of the open bitch class. There was a dog entered at this show named Bellman, by the North Fields Yorkshire kennels, a combination of Mr. Symonds of Salem, Mass., and Mr. Toon of Sheffield, England. This Bellman we think was the sire of the dam of Champion Merle Grady's dam, but he does not appear to have been shown. As he was entered at $1,000, while the same kennel's winner, Breda Bill, was only priced at $250, it is evident that, although entered as of unknown breeding, he must have been highly thought of. The Bellman we mean had won well in England in 1888 and 1889. Breda Bill was then bought by Mr. Harrison and won for him at a number of shows.

At New York in 1892 Dunmurry beat Breda Bill in the challenge class, and Mr. Comstock took first and second in open dogs with Boxer IV. and Hanover Boy. Third to them came Toon and Symonds Jack Briggs, a brother to Banty Norah, dam of Mr. Donner's future champion, Milton Droleen. By this time the breed had become so established that in 1893 it was advanced to the first-class rating of two challenge and two open classes, with one for puppies, and for these a total of thirty-eight entries was made, with no duplicates. There were many good ones in evidence, Jackanapes, owned by Colonel Hilton, taking first in dogs from Merle Grady. Jackanapes is a dog that had very few stud opportunities, but his name is found in many pedigrees and through various lines. Merle Grady later on won his championship and earned fame as the sire of Milton Droleen. Mr. Harrison had a new and good bitch in Candour that won first in her class and was afterwards shown by Dr. Jarrett.

A novice class was added to the schedule for New York in 1895, prior to which, however, we should mention that among the prominent winners in 1894 were Jack Briggs, Merle Grady, Jackanapes and Brickbat, Jr., in dogs, and Dunmurry, Candor and Hill Top Surprise, a daughter of Jackanapes, who won first at New York and other shows. At this show of 1895 the entry in challenge classes was excellent, Jackanapes winning in dogs and Dunmurry in bitches. In open dogs Brian O'K won in some mysterious way from Brigg's Best, but that was not the only peculiar decision, for Milton Droleen was put back to V.H.C. in the novice class. Mr. Taylor of England judged, and was quite out of his element with the Irish terriers.

The next event of importance was the addition of Mr. Oliver Ames to the list of exhibitors, together with Mr. W. W. Caswell, the former showing two good ones in Tory and Rum, and Mr. Caswell securing the renamed Willmount Highwayman, Endcliffe Matchbox and a few others. Leeds Muddler was also sent over by Mr. Ashton in 1898 and after being shown at Boston and New York was bought by Messrs Rodwell and Van Schaick, who a year later disposed of the dog to Mr. Howard Willetts and he was retired from public service. Milton Droleen, who had had a successful career in 1896 and 1897, was not in her usual good condition this spring and after being defeated at Boston was not shown at New York, permitting Rum and Mr. Caswell's Endcliffe Fusee to contest the honours in the Free for All at Madison Square Garden. In 1899 the roll of exhibitors was added to by the appearance of Mr. John I. Taylor of Boston, who purchased

111

Endcliffe Muddle from Toon and Thomas, and won three firsts at New York show. Mrs. Kernochan also showed as the Hempstead Kennel's, her best being Red Gem, which had a very successful career for many years, and after this show she purchased Lorton Belle, which Mr. Raper brought over and got second with her to Rum in the winners' class.

Lorton Belle did not hold her own for long, as at the next New York show she was beaten by both Red Gem and another new one of Mrs. Kernochan's, renamed Meadows Bridget. Inverness Shamrock, shown on this occasion by Mr. Raper and placed second to a dog called Ardle Topper, was then added to the Hempstead Kennels, which could now show an excellent kennel of four and won many specials with them. During this year Mr. George Thomas sold his Irish terriers to the Rushford Kennels and imported some new ones to add thereto, with the result that it soon became the most conspicuous contestant, and Mr. Bruckheimer's Masterpiece was the only terrier able to contend successfully against the Rushford's in 1902. Masterpiece came out at the show of the Pet Dog Club, held at the Metropolitan Opera House in November, 1900, and carried all before him, indeed, the dog was never beaten till he met Celtic Badger at New York in 1903. This was beyond doubt the best American bred dog of his day, or up to the present time. Indeed, not a few excellent terrier judges considered that on that occasion Celtic Badger was fortunate. We take no sides in the matter, but we are fully of the opinion that Badger improved quite a good deal during the following year, for he was slow in developing and when first shown at New York he was not so good in pasterns as he became later on. Mr. Jowett after judging Badger at the Boston show of 1905, told us that he was a greatly improved dog since he last saw him, adding that had they had any idea he would be the dog he then was it is extremely doubtful if he would ever have been allowed to come to this country. His criticism of Badger as nearly as we can recall his words were: "His head is not altogether what I want, for it is a little on the Taneous order in its straightness of the side lines. He has a good eye and carries his ears well. His neck is first-class and his back is good. His hind quarters could not be improved upon and he has just the kind of coat I like."

At the Philadelphia show of November, 1902, Mr. L. Loring Brooks of Boston showed a very nice puppy named Iroquois Muddle, which Mrs. Harding Davis bought later on, and won third to Badger and Masterpiece

RED HILLS KENNEL IRISH TERRIERS AT WORK

"HIGHLAND MUSIC"

By Sir Edwin Landseer, R. A

Painted probably about 1835.   Showing the ordinary run of Highland Terriers from which the Scottish was produced

at New York. Outside of these three the quality was not high. Drogheda should perhaps be excepted from that remark, for he was a very useful dog, with a keen expression somewhat lacking in Mrs. Kernochan's Inverness Shamrock, who was not a good shower. The new comers of 1904 included Selwonk Kudos and Red Hill's Doctor in dogs and a nice collection of bitches shown by Mr. E. S. Woodward in the name of the Raynham Kennels. His best bitches were better, we consider, than the dogs named, and he won many prizes with them wherever shown. They included Olivette, Radium, Surprise, all with the prefix of Raynham, and of these Olivette was the best, for though smaller than we usually see, she has excellent expression and for her inches shows much of the desirable racing outline.

In addition to Mr. L. Loring Brooks, who has been very prominent as a breeder for many years, Mr. S. P. Martin of Philadelphia has for some time been showing terriers of his own breeding, many of them very good in outline but rather too pointed in face, a fault which he is breeding out in a judicious manner, and as his entries show improvement he is and will continue to be a dangerous factor in home-bred and American-bred classes.

In the fall of 1904 a much needed impetus was given to this breed by the importation of a number of terriers by Mr. R. B. Adam of Buffalo, but at that time our judges' ideas were very much astray as to the right type of the Irish terrier and were of the opinion that the narrow Taneous head with heavy fluffy whiskers were the proper thing. The result was that as the new importations were flatter and wider in skull they were hardly done justice to, and Celtic Bella, a bitch that had for the previous six months defeated the pick of the dogs and bitches in England at every show she was exhibited at in England and Ireland, and twice won the Graham Cup, was roughly treated. To be sure of defeating the new comers other exhibitors also imported at very heavy expense, and as the only dogs that they could purchase as winners in England were similar in head to Mr. Adam's dogs, he at least had the satisfaction of thus demonstrating that his dogs were correct as to type of head.

Mr. Adam also strengthened his kennel for the New York show, with the result that when Mr. Jowett saw the turnout at Madison Square Garden last February he made no hesitation in saying that it was the best all-round exhibition of the breed he had seen anywhere for many years. On this occasion the new Rowsley Kennels won with the recently imported dog

Historian, next to him coming Mr. Adam's new puppy, Borthwick Benedict. High honours in the bitch division went to Mr. Munson Morris's new importation, Courtlandt Kate Kearney, who excels in front and body. Since the New York show England's best known dog, Straight Tip, has been imported by Mr. Gifford A. Cochrane, and only on one occasion has he been defeated since his arrival, and that by Historian, when Mr. Van Schaick judged at Brooklyn. Of this decision we are not justified in speaking, as we were at the Chicago show that week. Straight Tip is not always equally good. We know that horses sulk and decline to put forth their best efforts, and sometimes it may be that this dog does not care about doing his best to win, or to impress the judge. When he does show himself we know of no dog that can beat him for a certainty, and no person would be justified in saying off-hand that Badger could do so, for he has not met a dog of the calibre of Straight Tip at his best. Both are, however, getting on in years, and it is full time that some good new dog made his appearance.

There is every indication that we have got very near to an equal footing with English breeders in producing promising stock, for of late we have seen quite a number that show distinct advance in type and character from what has been the case previously. There is in this breed, as in some others where advance has been made, evidence that breeders have given up the idea of producing good ones from sires and dams from good parents and not themselves good, and when we reach that stage it is presumptive evidence that we may look for improvement.

We have already expressed some opinions regarding the desirable points in this breed and now repeat in condensed form what they were. We consider that the essentials to be regarded by the judge are: Type in body, meaning the racing outline characteristic of this breed; expression and shape of head, and given the former the latter can hardly be wrong, providing it is not narrow and round skulled; coat of correct texture is another essential, and that implies no fluffy whiskers on the lips; a closer approach to the standard weight should also be seen to by all judges, so that we may place the Irish terrier in his proper place as a red wire-haired dog somewhat larger than the fox terrier, and not a small Airedale.

The standard by which dogs are supposed to be judged is very old and was the work of a committee many being amateurs more or less ignorant of the breed from practical experience. A very much clearer and more easily understood text is the original description drawn up by

Mr. R. G. Ridgway and endorsed by twenty-four of the best known Irish breeders. It was this combination of breeders which induced Stonehenge to recognise the breed, though it was done reluctantly: "Head long and rather narrow across the skull [This is a comparative term suitable for that period, and the illustrations of the old winning terriers show what rather narrow then meant.—ED.]; flat, and perfectly free from stop or wrinkle. Muzzle long and rather pointed, but strong in make, with good black nose and free from loose flesh and chop. Teeth perfectly level and evenly set in good strong jaws. Ears, when uncut, small and filbert-shaped, and lying close to the head, colour of which is somewhat darker than rest of body; hair on ears short and free from fringe. Neck tolerably long and well arched. Legs moderately long, well set from shoulders, with plenty of bone and muscle; must be perfectly straight, and covered, like the ears and head, with the same texture of coat as the body, but not quite so long. Eyes small, keen and hazel colour. Feet strong, tolerably round, with toes well split up; most pure specimens have black toe nails. Chest muscular and rather deep, but should not be either full or wide. Body moderately long, with ribs well sprung; loin and back should show great strength and all well knit together. Coat must be hard, rough and wiry, in decided contradistinction to softness, shagginess, silkiness, and all parts perfectly free from lock or curl. Hair on head and legs not quite so long as rest of body. Colour most desired is red, and the brighter the colour the better. Next in order wheaten or yellow, and grey, but brindle is to be objected to, thereby showing intermixture of the bull breed."

In the standard founded upon the foregoing by the club of England and Ireland when it was organised, there are many indications of the fussy faddiness of the beginner in expounding inconsequential details, such as a negative penalty for white toe nails and for anything over a speck of white on chest. We were one of the aforesaid beginners, and of the entire ten committeemen in the English section probably one, possibly two, had bred a litter of Irish terriers, and two, George R. Krehl and James Watson, had exhibited. Of the Irish ten, four were well-known exhibitors. The English section particularly did a lot of amateurish things also in getting up stake conditions, which, with the conservatism of Englishmen, remain unaltered to this day and were adopted without thought or investigation by our Irish Terrier Club. The standard of both clubs is the same, and is as follows:

Head.—Long; skull flat and rather narrow between ears, getting slightly narrower towards the eye; free from wrinkle; stop hardly visible, except in profile. The jaw must be strong and muscular, but not too full in the cheek, and of a good punishing length. There should be a slight falling away below the eye, so as not to have a greyhound appearance. Hair on face of same description as on body, but short (about a quarter of an inch long), in appearance almost smooth and straight; a slight beard is the only longish hair (and it is long only in comparison with the rest) that is permissible, and that is characteristic.

Teeth.—Should be strong and level.

Lips.—Not so tight as a bull terrier's, but well-fitting, showing through the hair their black lining.

Nose.—Must be black.

Eyes.—A dark hazel colour, small, not prominent, and full of life, fire and intelligence.

Ears.—Small and V-shaped, of moderate thickness, set well on the head, and dropping forward closely to the cheek. The ear must be free of fringe, and the hair thereon shorter and darker in colour than the body.

Neck.—Should be of a fair length, and gradually widening towards the shoulders, well carried, and free of throatiness. There is generally a slight sort of frill visible at each side of the neck, running nearly to the corner of the ear.

Shoulders and chest.—Shoulders must be fine, long and sloping well into the back; the chest deep and muscular, but neither full nor wide.

Back and loin.—Body moderately long; back should be strong and straight, with no appearance of slackness behind the shoulders; the loin broad and powerful and slightly arched; ribs fairly sprung, rather deep than round, and well-ribbed back.

Hindquarters.—Should be strong and muscular, the thighs powerful, hocks near the ground, stifles moderately bent.

Stern. —Generally docked; should be free of fringe or feather, but well covered with rough hair, set on pretty high, carried gaily, but not over the back or curled.

117

Feet and legs.—Feet should be strong, tolerably round, and moderately small; toes arched and neither turned out nor in; black toe nails are most desirable. Legs moderately long, well set from the shoulders, perfectly straight with plenty of bone and muscle; the elbows working freely clear of the sides; pasterns short and straight, hardly noticeable. Both fore and hind legs should be moved straight forward when travelling, the stifles not turned outward, the legs free of feather and covered, like the head, with as hard a texture of coat as body, but not so long.

Coat.—Hard and wiry, free of softness or silkiness, not so long as to hide the outlines of the body, particularly in the hindquarters, straight and flat, no shagginess, and free of lock or curl.

Colour.—Should be "whole coloured," the most preferable being bright red, red, wheaten or yellow red. White sometimes appears on chest and feet; it is more objectionable on the latter than on the chest, as a speck of white on chest is frequently to be seen in all self-coloured breeds.

Size and symmetry.—The most desirable weight in show condition is, for a dog twenty-four pounds, and for a bitch twenty-two pounds. The dog must present an active, lively, lithe and wiry appearance; lots of substance, at the same time free of clumsiness, as speed and endurance, as well as power, are very essential. They must be neither "cloddy nor cobby," but should be framed on the "lines of speed," showing a graceful "racing outline."

Temperament.—Dogs that are very game are usually surly or snappish. The Irish terrier, as a breed, is an exception, being remarkably good tempered, notably so with mankind, it being admitted, however, that he is perhaps a little too ready to resent interference on the part of other dogs. There is a heedless, reckless pluck about the Irish terrier which is characteristic, and, coupled with the headlong dash, blind to all consequences, with which he rushes at his adversary, has earned for the breed the proud epithet of "The Dare Devils." When "off duty" they are characterised by a quiet, caress-inviting appearance, and when one sees them endearingly, timidly pushing their heads into their master's hands, it is difficult to realise that on occasion, at the "set-on," they can prove they have the courage of a lion, and will fight on to the last breath in their bodies. They develop an extraordinary devotion to, and have been known to track their masters almost incredible distances.

POSITIVE POINTS		NEGATIVE POINTS		
Head, ear and expression.	20	White nails, toes and feet.	.minus	10
Legs and feet.	15	Much white on chest	"	10
Neck	5	Dark shadings on face.	"	10
Shoulders and chest	10	Mouth undershot or cank-		
Back and loin	5	ered.	"	10
Hind quarters and stern.	10	Coat shaggy, curly or soft	"	10
Coat.	15	Uneven in colour	"	5
Colour	10			
Size and symmetry	10			
Total	100	Total		50

CH. PAYMASTER (SON), ERASMIC (MOTHER), PORCELAIN (DAUGHTER).
PROPERTY OF MISS LILIAN A. PAULL.

THE IRISH TERRIER.

BY ROBERT LEIGHTON.

" Though the last glimpse of Erin with sorrow I see,
Yet wherever thou art will seem Erin to me;
In exile thy bosom shall still be my home,
And thine eyes make my climate wherever we roam."
MOORE'S IRISH MELODIES.

THE dare-devil Irish Terrier has most certainly made his home in our bosom. There is no breed of dog more genuinely loved by those who have sufficient experience and knowledge to make the comparison. Other dogs have a larger share of innate wisdom, others are more æsthetically beautiful, others more peaceable; but our rufous friend has a way of winning into his owner's heart and making there an abiding place which is all the more secure because it is gained by sincere and undemonstrative devotion. Perhaps one likes him equally for his faults as for his merits. His very failings are due to his soldierly faithfulness and loyalty, to his too ardent vigilance in guarding the threshold, to his officious belligerence towards other canines who offend his sense of proprietorship in his master. His particular stature may have some influence in his success as a chum. He is just tall enough to rest his chin upon one's knee and look up with all his soul into one's eyes. Whatever be the secret of his attraction—whether it is merely a subtle Irish blarney that conquers, or a spontaneous worship of the being who is to him instead of a god—'tis certain that he has the Hibernian art of compelling affection and forgiveness, and that he makes one value him, not for the beauty of his ruddy raiment, the straightness of his forelegs, the set of his eye and ear, the levelness of his back, or his ability

120

to win prizes, but rather for his true and trusty heart, that exacts no return and seeks no recompense. He may be but an indifferent specimen of his kind, taken in as a stranger at the gates; but when at length the inevitable time arrives, as it does all too soon in canine nature, one then discovers how surely one has been harbouring an angel unawares.

Statistics would probably show that in numbers the Fox-terrier justifies the reputation of being a more popular breed, and the Scottish Terrier is no doubt a formidable competitor for public esteem. It is safe, however, to say that the Irish Terrier shares with these the distinction of being one of the three most popular dogs in the British Isles.

This fact taken into consideration, it is interesting to reflect that thirty years ago the Dare-Devil was virtually unknown in England. Idstone, in his book on dogs, published in 1872, did not give a word of mention to the breed, and dog shows had been instituted sixteen years before a class was opened for the Irish Terrier. The dog existed, of course, in its native land. It may indeed be almost truthfully said to have existed " as long as that country has been an island."

About the year 1875, experts were in dispute over the Irish Terrier, and many averred that his rough coat and length of hair on forehead and muzzle were indubitable proof of Scotch blood. His very expression, they said, was Scotch. But the argument was quelled by more knowing disputants on the other side, who claimed that Ireland had never been without her terrier, and that she owed no manner of indebtedness to Scotland for a dog whose every hair was essentially Irish.

In the same year at a show held in Belfast a goodly number of the breed were brought together, notable among them being Mr. D. O'Connell's Slasher, a very good-looking wire-coated working terrier, who is said to have excelled as a field and water dog. Slasher was lint white in colour, and reputed to be descended from a pure white strain. Two other terriers of the time were

Mr. Morton's Fly (the first Irish Terrier to gain a championship) and Mr. George Jamison's Sport. These three dogs were heard of with curiosity in England, and in The Live Stock Journal of August 20th, 1875, an engraved portrait of Sport was published. The illustration was received with great interest, representing as it assuredly did a genuine and typical Irish Terrier. In the portrait the dog's muzzle is seen to be somewhat snipy; he is light in the eye, but his ear carriage is good and his shape of head, his limbs, body, stern and coat are admirable. From all that one can gather concerning him, he seems to have been, in reality, a far better example of his intrepid breed than any that were put above him in competition—better, for instance, than the same owner's Banshee, who died a champion, and at least equal to Mr. W. Graham's Sporter or Mr. E. F. Despard's Tanner, by whom he was frequently beaten.

The prominent Irish Terriers of the 'seventies varied considerably in type. Stinger, who won the first prize at Lisburn in 1875, was long-backed and short-legged, with a " dark blue grizzle coloured back, tan legs, and white turned-out feet." The dam of Mr. Burke's Killeney Boy was a rough black and tan, a combination of colours which was believed to accompany the best class of coats. Brindles were not uncommon. Some were tall on the leg, some short. Some were lanky and others cobby. Many were very small. There were classes given at a Dublin show in 1874 for Irish Terriers under 9 lb. weight.

Jamison's Sport is an important dog historically, for various reasons. He was undoubtedly more akin to our present type than any other Irish Terrier of his time of which there is record. His dark ears were uncropped at a period when cropping was general; his weight approximated to our modern average. He was an all coloured red, and his legs were of a length that would not now be seriously objected to. But in his day he was not accepted as typical, and he was not particularly successful in the show ring. The distinguished terrier of

121

his era was Burke's Killeney Boy, to whom, and to Mr. W. Graham's bitch Erin, with whom he was mated, nearly all the pedigrees of the best Irish Terriers of to-day date back. Erin was said to be superior in all respects to any of her breed previous to 1880. In her first litter by Killeney Boy were Play Boy, Pretty Lass, Poppy, Gerald, Pagan II., and Peggy, every one of whom became famous. More than one of these showed the black markings of their granddam, and their progeny for several generations were apt to throw back to the black-and-tan, grey, or brindle colouring. Play Boy and Poppy were the best of Erin's first litter. The dog's beautiful ears, which were left as Nature made them, were transmitted to his son Bogie Rattler, who was sire of Bachelor and Benedict, the latter the most successful stud dog of his time. Poppy had a rich red coat, and this colour recurred with fair regularity in her descendants. Red, which had not at first been greatly appreciated, came gradually to be the accepted colour of an Irish Terrier's jacket. Occasionally it tended towards flaxen ; occasionally to a deep rich auburn ; but the black and brindle were so rigidly bred out that by the year 1890, or thereabout, they very seldom recurred. Nowadays it is not often that any other colour than red is seen in a litter of Irish Terriers, although a white patch on the breast is frequent, as it is in all self-coloured breeds.

In addition to the early celebrities already named, Extreme Carelessness, Michael, Brickbat, Poppy II., Moya Doolan, Straight Tip, and Gaelic have taken their places in the records of the breed, while yet more recent Irish Terriers who have achieved fame have been Mrs. Butcher's Bawn Boy

MR. GEORGE JAMISON'S SPORT (1875).

and Bawn Beauty, Mr. Wallace's Treasurer, Mr. S. Wilson's Bolton Woods Mixer, Dr. Smyth's Sarah Kidd, and Mr. C. J. Barnett's Breda Muddler. Of these Sarah Kidd was, perhaps, the most perfect, but unquestionably the most famous was Bolton Woods Mixer. Probably no dog of any breed has in its career been more familiar to the public. In his prime he was to be seen at almost every important dog show, always occupying a prominent position. He must have earned quite a respectable income for his master. Indeed, he was known as "Sam Wilson's Bread-winner." Over two thousand first prizes, cups, medals, and championships were credited to him, and it is not to be wondered at that Mr. Wilson refused as much as £700 for him. Mixer lived to a good old age, for at the time of his death from pneumonia and blood poisoning, in April, 1907, he was in his twelfth year.

Naturally in the case of a breed which has departed from its original type, discussions were frequent before a standard of perfection for the Irish Terrier was fixed. His size and weight, the length or shortness of his limbs, the carriage of his tail, the form of his skull and muzzle, the colour and texture of his coat were the subjects of controversy. It was considered at one juncture that he was being bred too big, and at another that he was being brought too much to resemble a red wire-hair Fox-terrier. When once the black marking on his body had been eliminated no one seems to have desired that it should be restored. Red was acknowledged to be the one and only colour for an Irish Terrier. But some held that the correct red should be deep auburn, and others that wheaten colour was the tone to be aimed at. A medium shade between the two extremes is now generally preferred. As to size, it should be about midway between that of the Airedale and the Fox-terrier, represented by a weight of from 22 to 27 lb.

The two breeds just mentioned are, as a rule, superior to the Irish Terrier in front,

MR. S. WILSON'S **CH** BOLTON WOODS MIXER. WINNER OF TWO THOUSAND PRIZES.

legs, and feet, but in the direction of these points great improvements have recently been observable. The heads of our Irish Terriers have also been brought nearer to a level of perfection, chiselled to the desired degree of leanness, with the determined expression so characteristic of the breed, and with the length, squareness, and strength of muzzle which formerly were so difficult to find. This squareness of head and jaw is an important point to be considered when choosing an Irish Terrier. In the best specimens of the breed, the muzzle, skull, and neck, when seen in profile, exactly fit within an imaginary rectangular frame, thus :—

Opinions differ in regard to slight details of this terrier's conformation, but the official description, issued by the Irish Terrier Club, supplies a guide upon which the uncertain novice may implicitly depend :—

1. Head.—Long ; skull flat, and rather narrow between ears, getting slightly narrower towards the eye ; free from wrinkles ; stop hardly visible except in profile. The jaw must be strong and muscular, but not too full in the cheek, and of a good punishing length. There should be a slight falling away below the eye, so as not to have a Greyhound appearance. Hair on face of same description as on body, but short (about a quarter of an inch long), in appearance almost smooth and straight ; a slight beard is the only longish hair (and it is only long in comparison with the rest) that is permissible, and this is characteristic.

2. Teeth.—Should be strong and level.

3. Lips.—Not so tight as a Bull-Terrier's, but well-fitting, showing through the hair their black lining.

4. Nose.—Must be black.

5. Eyes.—A dark hazel colour, small, not prominent, and full of life, fire, and intelligence.

6. Ears.—Small and V-shaped, of moderate thickness, set well on the head, and dropping forward closely to the cheek. The ear must be free of fringe, and the hair thereon shorter and darker in colour than the body.

7. Neck.—Should be of a fair length, and gradually widening towards the shoulders, well carried, and free of throatiness. There is generally a slight sort of frill visible at each side of the neck, running nearly to the corner of the ear.

8. Shoulders and Chest.—Shoulders must be fine, long, and sloping well into the back ; the chest deep and muscular, but neither full nor wide.

9. Back and Loin.—Body moderately long ; back should be strong and straight, with no appearance of slackness behind the shoulders ; the loin broad and powerful, and slightly arched ; ribs fairly sprung, rather deep than round, and well ribbed back.

10. Hindquarters.—Should be strong and muscular, thighs powerful, hocks near ground, stifles moderately bent.

11. Stern.—Generally docked ; should be free of fringe or feather, but well covered with rough hair, set on pretty high, carried gaily, but not over the back or curled.

12. Feet and Legs.—Feet should be strong, tolerably round, and moderately small ; toes arched, and neither turned out nor in ; black toe nails most desirable. Legs moderately long, well set from the shoulders, perfectly straight, with plenty of bone and muscle ; the elbows working freely clear of the sides ; pasterns short and straight, hardly noticeable. Both fore and hind legs should be moved straight forward when travelling, the stifles not turned outwards, the legs free of feather, and covered, like the head, with as hard a texture of coat as body, but not so long.

13. Coat.—Hard and wiry, free of softness or silkiness, not so long as to hide the outlines of the body, particularly in the hindquarters, straight and flat, no shagginess, and free of lock or curl.

14. Colour.—Should be "whole coloured," the most preferable being bright red, red, wheaten, or yellow red. White sometimes appears on chest and feet ; it is more objectionable on the latter than on the chest, as a speck of white on chest is frequently to be seen in all self-coloured breeds.

15. Size and Symmetry.—The most desirable weight in show condition is, for a dog 24 lb., and for a bitch 22 lb. The dog must present an active, lively, lithe, and wiry appearance ; lots of substance, at the same time free of clumsiness, as speed and endurance, as well as power, are very essential. They must be neither cloddy nor cobby, but should be framed on the lines of speed, showing a graceful racing outline.

16. Temperament. —Dogs that are very game are usually surly or snappish. The Irish Terrier as a breed is an exception, being remarkably good-tempered, notably so with mankind, it being admitted, however, that he is perhaps a little too ready to resent interference on the part of other dogs. There is a heedless, reckless pluck about the Irish Terrier which is characteristic, and, coupled with the headlong dash, blind to all consequences, with which he rushes at his adversary, has earned for the breed the proud epithet of "The Dare-Devils." When "off duty" they are characterised by a quiet, caress-inviting appearance, and when one sees them endearingly, timidly pushing their heads into their masters' hands, it is difficult to realise that on occasions, at the "set on," they can prove they have the courage of a lion, and will fight unto the last breath in their bodies. They develop an extraordinary devotion to and have been known to track their masters almost incredible distances.

MR. J. J. HOLGATE'S HAUTBOY
BY STRAIGHT BOY—KITTY.

It is difficult to refer to particular Irish Terriers of to-day without making invidious distinctions. There are so many excellent examples of the breed that a list even of those who have gained championship honours would be formidable. But one would hardly hesitate to head the list with the name of Ch. Paymaster, a dog of rare and almost superlative quality and true Irish Terrier character. Paymaster is the property of Miss Lilian Paull, of Weston-super-Mare, who bred him from her beautiful bitch Erasmic from Ch. Breda Muddler, the sire of many of the best. Miss Paull's kennel has also produced notably good specimens of the breed in Postman (litter brother to Paymaster), President, and Postboy. Side by side with Ch. Paymaster, Mr. F. Clifton's Ch. Mile End Barrister might be placed. It would need a council of perfection, indeed, to decide which is the better dog of the two. Very high in the list, also, would come Mr. Henry Ridley's Ch. Redeemer. And among bitches one would name certainly Mr. Gregg's Ch. Belfast Erin, Mr. Clifton's Ch. Charwoman, Mr. Everill's Ch. Erminie, and Mr. J. S. McComb's Ch. Beeston Betty. These are but half a dozen, but they represent the highest level of excellence that has yet been achieved by scientific breeding in Irish Terrier type.

Breeding up to the standard of excellence necessary in competition in dog shows has doubtless been the agent which has brought the Irish Terrier to its present condition

MISS LILIAN A. PAULL'S CH. PAYMASTER
BY CH. BREDA MUDDLER—ERASMIC.

of perfection, and it is the means by which the general dog owning public is most surely educated to a practical knowledge of what is a desirable and what an undesirable dog to possess. But, after all, success in the show ring is not the one and only thing to be aimed at, and the Irish Terrier is not to be regarded merely as the possible winner of prizes. He is above all things a dog for man's companionship, and in this capacity he takes a favoured place. He has the great advantage of being equally suitable for town and country life. In the home he requires no pampering ; he has a good, hardy constitution, and when once

he has got over the ills incidental to puppyhood—worms and distemper—he needs only to be judiciously fed, kept reasonably clean, and to have his fill of active exercise. If he is taught to be obedient and of gentlemanly habit, there is no better house dog. He is naturally intelligent and easily trained. Although he is always ready to take his own part, he is not quarrelsome, but remarkably good-tempered and a safe associate of children. Perhaps with his boisterous spirits he is prone sometimes to be overzealous in the pursuit of trespassing tabbies and in assailing the ankles of intruding butcher boys and officious postmen. These characteristics come from his sense of duty, which is strongly developed, and careful training will make him discriminative in his assaults.

Very justly is he classed among the sporting dogs. He is a born sportsman, and of his pluck it were superfluous to speak. Fear is unknown to him. In this characteristic as in all others, he is truly a son of Erin, and, like his military countrymen, he excels in strategy and tactics. Watch him when hunting on his own on a rabbit warren ; see him when a badger is about ; follow his movements when on the scent of a fox ; take note of his activity in the neighbourhood of an otter's holt ; observe his alertness even at the very mention of rats ! As a ratter the Irish Terrier has no rival. Mr. Ridgway's story of Antrim Jess illustrates both the terrier's ratting capabilities and its resourceful strategy. A bank was being bored for the wily vermin. One bolted. Jess had him almost before he had cleared his hole. Then came another and another, so fast that the work was getting too hot even for Jess ; when a happy thought seemed to strike her, and while in the act of killing a very big one, she leaned down and jammed her shoulder against the hole and let them out one by one, nipping them in succession until eighteen lay dead at her feet !

IRISH TERRIERS.

ALTHOUGH Irish Terriers had been bred in Ireland for many years before classes had been previously given for them at Irish Shows, it was not until 1876 that they were first officially recognised and given a place to themselves in the Kennel Club Stud Book.

Birmingham is believed to have been the first English Show which catered for Irish Terriers, and among the earliest exhibitors on this side of the water were Messrs. Carey, Krehl, Barnett and Graham, all of whose names are household words in the breed, and to whose keenness in engineering and improving the breed, there will always remain a debt of gratitude.

As might be expected, they originally varied very considerably in conformation and weight, and their coats were of many colours, including brindle, black and tan, grizzled, red, etc It is, however, safe to say that from the before-mentioned date onwards, the colour settled down to wheaten, red wheaten, and the desired golden red of the present day, which is usually the soundest and most honest coat of all, and not requiring improper preparation for Show purposes.

To speculate as to the class of dogs they originated from, the probability is that a rough-coated Fox-Terrier, a Black-and-Tan, a Bedlington, and possibly a Bulldog, all had a hand, more or less, in producing the breed, and to a certain extent the characteristics of temperament of the two last-named still remain in a modified form. On the other hand it may be that, being indigenous to Ireland, and in close contact with their masters, they gradually acquired the pluck and determination, with a readiness to be there when there is a scent of battle about, for which the country is renowned. For many years it was the fashion to crop their ears, as it was supposed to smarten their appearance and lend additional keenness to their expression, but apart from the cruelty the operation involved, it was obviously an artificial way of bringing about that which intelligent breeding has accomplished naturally. The Irish Terrier Club was the first to abolish cropping (in 1887), and the Kennel Club made a rule prohibiting the exhibition of dogs cropped after December, 1889.

Probably the late Mr. Geo. Krehl, with the aid of his then powerful paper, *The Stock-Keeper*, combined with his clever pen, did most towards bringing the breed to the front and winning recruits to the Irish Terrier Fancy. As a breeder of Irish Terriers, however, he was not successful, but he was always prepared to buy good ones, and he showed them with success. Others whose names were associated with Irish Terriers in the early days as breeders and exhibitors were Messrs. Geo. Jamieson, Waterhouse, Backhouse, and later on came Mr. Geo. Mayall, who originally bought pluckily and has bred some of the best; Mr. E. A. Weiner, whose name will go down to posterity as the breeder of Ch. Brickbat; and Messrs. Yarr, Breakell, Mrs. Butcher, Messrs. T. Wallace, F. M. Jowett, F. Clifton, H. Benner, H. J. Twamley, S. Wilson, R. S. Knox, Miss Paull, H. Ridley, etc., being the best known names up to date. There are of course other staunch Irish Terrier Fanciers, whose names for the moment the writer forgets, but who have done yeoman service, and he must ask their forgiveness for not being able to mention them. Irish Terriers are essentially good companions under all circumstances, as they easily adapt themselves to any surroundings, and when accustomed to children they are absolutely reliable with them. No dog has greater intelligence or more loyalty. In fact, if they have a fault—and if it is a fault—they are inclined to guard their masters and their home too jealously. Like the proverbial Bristol man, they always seem to "sleep with one eye open," and be alive to any movement in their vicinity whether they are on a hearthrug or in a kennel. Whatever is going on they like to take part in it, and they have the happy knack of insinuating themselves into the affections of their owners whether they have committed offences or not. The writer considers there is no more charming "pal" than an Irish Terrier bitch. He does not wish to say anything against dogs, and most people prefer the male sex, but he always thinks bitches in any breed are better companions, as they are more responsive, quieter, and not so fond of "exploring."

It is essential in every breed that a Club should be formed to look after its interests, and the Irish Terrier Club was established in 1879. It has always been recognised

128

as one of the leading Specialist Clubs, the Secretarial duties having been ably carried out by Dr. R. B. Carey practically since its formation. It supports all the leading Shows with Special Prizes, and has a list of twenty-five Judges, which are elected by the members annually.

Other Irish Terrier Clubs have since been established, which, however, cater principally for the smaller Shows in the matter of Special Prizes :—The Irish Terrier Club of Scotland ; the Leinster Irish Terrier Club ; the Junior Irish Terrier Club ; the London and South of England Irish Terrier Club ; the North of England Irish Terrier Club, and the Ulster Irish Terrier Club.

A Club Show is now held by the Irish Terrier Club annually, the first of which was started in connection with the Bristol Show in 1897.

It is generally admitted that, taking it all in all, the description and scale of points laid down by the Irish Terrier Club some years ago, cannot easily be improved upon, except perhaps in respect of weight, which is a little under the mark for the stamp of dog described and most appreciated, but possibly if the weight were fixed at a higher point, it would lead to liberties being taken and be an excuse for showing still larger dogs than are exhibited now, which should be prevented at any cost, as some are much too large and leggy now if there is to be the wide difference between an "Irishman" and an Airedale, and there should be. To be prejudiced however, or condemn a dog because his weight exceeds the standard weight by two or three pounds is wrong, as some of our most compact and typical specimens are astonishingly heavy without being big, by reason of their bone and substance, which is what is wanted ; whereas a whippety small boned specimen, higher on the leg, and altogether looking lanky, will probably not exceed 24 lbs.

It was, however, never intended, and never will be, that Judges should religiously follow the Irish Terrier Club's recommendations in every particular point, and weigh up the value of each when making the awards, as such a course would take too much time and probably end in hopeless confusion and indecision. Judging dogs has never yet been successfully carried out by going on the "rule of thumb" principle, and all that can be reasonably expected, is that the Judge should have a good general knowledge of the breed, and the points most to be encouraged, have no fads nor prejudices, and with an open mind fearlessly record his decision according to his lights and *the way the dogs appear before him at the moment.* We shall never all agree and it would be a bad thing if we did, because the interest attaching to the different verdicts of different Judges would be done away with, and Dog Shows would suffer in consequence.

The following is the Irish Terrier Club's description and standard of points :—

DESCRIPTIVE PARTICULARS.

Head—Long : skull flat, and rather narrow between ears, getting slightly narrower towards the eye ; free from wrinkles ; stop hardly visible except in profile. The jaw must be strong and muscular, but not too full in the cheek, and of a good punishing length. There should be a slight falling away below the eye, so as not to have a greyhound appearance. Hair on face of same description as on body, but short (about a quarter of an inch long) in appearance almost smooth and straight ; a slight beard is the only longish hair (and it is only long in comparison with the rest) that is permissible, and that is characteristic. *Teeth*—Should be strong and level. *Lips*—Not so tight as a bull terrier's, but well-fitting, showing through the hair their black lining. *Nose*—Must be black. *Eyes*—A dark hazel colour, small, not prominent, and full of life, fire, and intelligence. *Ears*—Small and V-shaped, of moderate thickness, set well on the head, and dropping forward closely to the cheek. The ear must be free of fringe, and the hair thereon shorter and darker in colour than the body. *Neck*—Should be of a fair length and gradually widening towards the shoulders, well carried, and free of throatiness. There is generally a slight sort of frill visible at each side of the neck, running nearly to the corner of the ear. *Shoulder and Chest*—Shoulders must be fine, long, and sloping well into the back; the chest deep and muscular, but neither full nor wide. *Back and Loin*—Body moderately

CH. BEESTON BETTY.

long; back should be strong and straight, with no appearance of slackness behind the shoulders; the loin broad and powerful and slightly arched; ribs fairly sprung, rather deep than round, and well ribbed back. *Hind Quarters*—Should be strong and muscular, the thighs powerful, hocks near the ground, stifles moderately bent. *Stern*—Generally docked; should be free of fringe or feather, but well covered with

131

rough hair, set on pretty high, carried gaily, but not over the back or curled. *Feet and Legs*—Feet should be strong, tolerably round, and moderately small toes arched, and neither turned out nor in; black toe nails most desirable. Legs moderately long, well set from the shoulders, perfectly straight, with plenty of bone and muscle; the elbows working freely clear of the sides; pasterns short and straight, hardly noticeable. Both fore and hind legs should be moved straight forward when travelling, the stifles not turned outwards, the legs free of feather, and covered, like the head, with as hard a texture of coat as body, but not so long. *Coat*—Hard and wiry, free of softness or silkiness, not so long as to hide the outlines of the body, particularly in the hind quarters, straight and flat, no shagginess and free of lock or curl. *Colour*—Should be "whole coloured," the most preferable being bright red, red-wheaten, or yellow red. White sometimes appears on chest and feet; it is more objectionable on the latter than on the chest, as a speck of white on chest is frequently to be seen in all self-coloured breeds. *Size and Symmetry*—The most desirable weight in Show condition is, for a dog 24 lbs., and for a bitch 22 lbs. The dog must present an active, lively, lithe and wiry appearance; lots of substance, at the same time free of clumsiness, as speed and endurance, as well as power, are very essential. They must be neither "cloddy nor cobby," but should be framed on "the lines of speed," showing a graceful "racing outline." *Temperament*—Dogs that are very game are usually surly or snappish. The Irish Terrier as a breed is an exception, being remarkably good tempered, notably so with mankind, it being admitted, however, that he is perhaps a little too ready to resent interference on the part of other dogs. There is a heedless reckless pluck about the Irish Terrier which is characteristic, and, coupled with the headlong dash, blind to all consequences, with which he rushes at his adversary, has earned for the breed the proud epithet of "The Dare Devils." When "off duty"

132

they are characterised by a quiet caress-inviting appearance, and when one sees them endearingly, timidly pushing their heads into their master's hands, it is difficult to realise that on occasions, at the "set on," they can prove they have the courage of a lion, and will fight unto the last breath in their bodies. They develop an extraordinary devotion to, and have been known to track their masters almost incredible distances.

Irish Terriers are hardy dogs and not difficult to breed, which is a great thing with the average Dog Fancier, who is only able to devote a certain amount of spare time to his hobby.

Like all other breeds, bitches should be well but judiciously fed when in whelp. It is highly undesirable to leave more than six puppies for a bitch to bring up, and if there are more, they should be either put to a foster mother (which is very often difficult to arrange), or destroyed; the latter plan being in my opinion the more satisfactory and the least expensive. The trouble, however, is in deciding which of them should be put out of the way, but as a general rule it is best to keep those which appear to have the strongest forefaces, the smallest ears, and the straightest and least fluffy coats. If they are kept until their eyes are open, the bluest eyes are most likely to turn out to be the best coloured eventually. Nothing has been said about the colour of their coats at this age because this often changes considerably as they grow older, and a puppy at a few weeks old which has a lot of black in its coat will usually shed it, and the next coat will be of the correct colour. If, however, a puppy shows a wave in its coat when it is born, the probability is that when matured the waviness or curliness will take a more pronounced form, which class of coat is generally deprecated by Irish Terrier Fanciers, as it detracts from the appearance, and, to put it mildly, needs "special preparation" in skilful hands in order to minimise the fault.

A judicious dock adds greatly to the appearance of any

Terrier (whose tail it is customary to shorten) and assuming the head is of the desired length, in order to get a symmetrical outline, it requires balancing at the stern with a tail not too short nor too long, inclining to the latter of the two.

Some breeders leave puppies with their dam until she weans them herself, but this is not desirable, especially if it is a Show bitch, as they pull her out of shape too much, and about six weeks is quite long enough. For the last two weeks it is well to assist the bitch by taking her away at intervals and feeding the puppies with carefully prepared and digestible food, giving it time to digest, before she is put back to them. On the other hand, puppies will often flourish which have gradually taken to sharing their mother's meals and without any special precautions being taken. So perhaps the safest plan is to follow out the instructions given on " Food and Feeding " by a contributor in another part of the ENCYCLOPÆDIA, because practically all puppies (with the exception perhaps of Toy dogs) should be fed somewhat similarly, of course having a due regard to the fact that a Terrier is being reared which, when developed, must not be too large.

The mating of Irish Terriers with success is by no means easy, and one of the first things to be considered is the points of your bitch. Putting the question of pedigree and theoretical breeding aside for one moment, it is better that a brood bitch should have no very radical faults which are likely to be handed down, and possess a coat of really good texture, not a suspicion of silky hair anywhere (her dam and grand-dam having possessed the same, if it can be managed) and good legs and feet (avoid weak ankles, and a slight absence of bone may be forgiven, if what is there is straight), a moderate-sized ear, a fairly clean skull, and whether the bitch is on the large or small side is not important, although the small is preferable.

In a stud dog you particularly want a good length of

head, good ears, a small dark eye, good shoulders and bone to the feet, with of course a hard coat. If he possesses other good qualities all the better, but in any case, used to the class of bitch described, the result should not be altogether unsatisfactory, and at least the right path is being taken to get what is wanted sooner or later.

The mistake so many people make is in mating their bitches to dogs, simply because they see the dogs are prize-winners or through artistic descriptions in Stud advertisements by their enterprising owners, and quite regardless of whether they are suitable to the bitches or not. This kind of haphazard breeding can but end in disappointment in nine cases out of ten.

There is no need to go into the theory of breeding dogs on scientific principles, as the subject is very ably dealt with in another part of the ENCYCLOPÆDIA, and although the writer has offered simple and elementary advice on mating as the result of his own experience, he strongly recommends that the article on breeding referred to, be carefully perused and as far as possible acted upon.

If it can be managed, puppies should be sent to "walk" for a few months at country cottages, where they are practically never shut up. This mode of living makes them hardy, and they grow straighter and better than if they were fed ever so well in kennels, where their exercise must be to a certain extent restricted. They should, however, be periodically visited—say once a month—in order to see if they are progressing favourably and are properly cared for. Under these conditions, they shake off distemper much more easily than if you had them at home with other dogs, no matter how carefully you nurse them. Whether it is the freedom, or the fresh air, or the absence of "sovereign remedies," it is difficult to say. There is one other thing to be suggested, which is that, where it can be managed, it is best to choose cottages where there are no children, as there are more scraps about and they are very much better

135

looked after, becoming part of the family. When puppies come in from "walk," say at six or seven months old, it will soon be seen whether they have made their growth properly, or if they require forcing in any way, and in the latter case, there is nothing better than a few ounces of minced raw beef a day after their ordinary food. Indeed, where they are not doing well at all ages, from eight weeks old and upwards, a small quantity of minced beef has a wonderful effect.

As has been said before, Irish Terriers are hardy dogs, and in health should require no more warmth than that given by a bed of straw, which should be frequently changed, and of course their kennels should be dry and weather proof. This remark applies to dogs which are always kept out of doors.

For sporting purposes, it is said that the colour of Irish Terriers' coats is against them—say for rabbiting—and there is some truth in it, but after all, it must be a poor sportsman who loses his head sufficiently to fire at his dog in mistake for a rabbit. If properly trained in their youth, they can work a hedge-row as well as any kind of Terrier, and it is a treat to see them chase a rabbit across a field in its own country, although it is only occasionally that they succeed in catching one; nevertheless, they have "a run for the money" and give their owners some excitement in a legitimate way. They are also great water dogs and rare ratters, and in fact will face anything if they are brought up in sporting surroundings; but if not, they can be made lap-dogs without much trouble, in the same way as every other Terrier.

Irish Terriers formerly were used a good deal for rabbit coursing, on account of being the most speedy Terrier, but now-a-days we find that this unsportsmanlike form of entertainment is pretty well played out, for nothing can be more cruel than trapping and taking a timid little animal like a rabbit, miles away from its own locality and turning it loose in a large field, with no haven of rest in sight, and a dog at its heels, urged on by a shouting mob.

Irish Terriers are also very popular abroad for sporting purposes, especially in India, where a great many are sent, and they are quite part of an Army officer's outfit, particularly as they can often be sold for large figures to Indian potentates. They are well to the front in other countries, and a dog which won a considerable number of prizes in England, belonging to a friend of mine, went through the last Egyptian War and proved himself one of the most alert sentries at his master's tent. He was never surprised, and left his mark on more than one coloured trespasser. Americans, however, are the largest purchasers of Irish Terriers at high prices, but they want them principally for Show purposes.

To keep Irish Terriers for Show and at the same time to use the Show specimens for sporting purposes is obviously impossible if they are to appear to the best advantage in the Ring. It is therefore folly, if there is a desire to win prizes, not to do one's utmost to put the dog down in the Show Ring to the best possible advantage. To do this it is necessary to judiciously feed and give plenty of walking exercise beforehand, so that the dog gets well upon his feet and has a hard, healthy appearance. The coat, however, plays an important part in the general appearance, and special attention must be given to it in the shape of regularly combing and brushing. The tendency to show Irish Terriers short of coat for the sake of giving them a clearer outline, or more probably to disguise what the texture of coat really is when grown, should be severely penalized.

The mistake so many make, and what brings about improper preparation, is a desire to show a dog too frequently and for too long together. No Wire-haired Terrier can be honestly shown to advantage with the same coat for an indefinite period, that is, if it has a coat worthy of the name. It is always growing, and will gradually get too long for a smart appearance in the Show Ring if "barbering" is not resorted to. It changes twice a year, and will remain in Show condition for a reasonable time. After that, give the dog a rest and keep him at home until the time comes round when he is fit to show again, after shedding his coat naturally. The new coat will be ever so much better and more even, if the old coat has not been plucked in patches.

In the Ring an Irish Terrier should be bright, lively and in every way ready to hold his own if necessary, but not encouraged to fight with his next door neighbour. Fighting in a Ring is a nuisance to everybody, and a dog straining at his lead with lips turned back, springing at this dog and that dog, always appears to be at his worst. Further than this, it gives those outside the Ring who might otherwise be fascinated with his unique appearance, an erroneous idea of his character, which is as gentle as any Terrier's if he has been properly brought up. Education on the lead, with a tasty bit of food in the hand, can do a lot towards making him show well, and in this way the true keen and intelligent expression brought out, is far better than the sour and savage look when endeavouring to fight.

It is common knowledge that practically all our best Irish Terriers trace their descent from "Killiney Boy" and "Erin." To enumerate all the good dogs and bitches produced since would be an impossible task, but mention may be made of a few of the most notable.

In dogs : Playboy, Gripper, Pagan II., Bogie Rattler, Bachelor, Benedict, Brickbat, Pilgrim, Breda Mixer, Ted Malone, Bawnboy, Breda Muddler, Treasurer, Checkmate, Bolton Woods Mixer, Mile End Muddler, Straight Tip, Mile End Barrister, Paymaster, and Redeemer.

In bitches : Biddy III., Extreme Carelessness, Droleen, Sarah Kidd, Belfast Erin, Charwoman, Charmian, Beeston Belle, Bawn Beauty, Erminie, Kate Kearney, Crowgil Moira, and Beeston Betty.

To single out the most successful stud dogs since the days of Brickbat, which obviously most affect those of the present day, Breda Mixer will come first, and on one side or the other, he has played an important part in almost every dog named, since his time, thus showing that he must have handed down his own great qualities and the value of his blood. Breda Mixer was bred by the late Mr. William Graham, of Belfast—undoubtedly the cleverest fancier of the breed we have ever had. This is proved by the fact that all the best dogs we have now are descendants from his strain.

I mention Breda Muddler next, because he has directly sired a larger proportion of high-class dogs than any other Irish Terrier. He was bred by Mr. Geo. Mayall, who, when he took up the breed, very wisely followed

Mr. Graham's line, and acquired from him some of his best dogs, with satisfactory results. Breda Muddler is by Breda Mixer *ex* Breda Iris, who was not a show specimen, but a nice little bitch, and bred a number of good ones. The litter which included Breda Muddler was an exceptional one, and among other prize winners in it was Ch. Checkmate, a taking little dog which won a lot of prizes, but did not prove valuable at stud, probably because he was never a dog with much stamina.

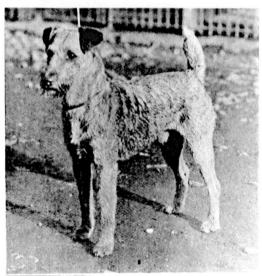

CH. PAYMASTER.

Another good one was Bolton Woods Mixer (by Breda Mixer *ex* Saskatchewan). He was bought at a small show as a puppy by Mr. Samuel Wilson, and in his time probably won more prizes than any dog of any breed that ever existed, which is something to boast of. He also retained his show form in a wonderful way for an unusually long time. As a stud dog his opportunities were enormous, and he was the sire of many good ones, but also of many bad coated ones, a fault which is attributable to his breeding on his dam's side.

Mile End Muddler—by Breda Muddler *ex* Burma, bred by Mr. C. J. Barnett—has proved himself a valuable stud dog, and I always regard him as one of the best, as he combines high quality in himself with unimpeachable blood on both sides.

The last dog to be commented upon is much younger, and has hardly had time as yet to prove conclusively the high opinion held about him by some as a dog to breed from, although so far his stock have been very successful. This refers to Paymaster, bred and owned by Miss L. A. Paull. He is by Breda Muddler *ex* Erasmic, thus introducing on his dam's side the blood of an entirely different—at least for some generations—but desirable strain, which is so essential when such a large proportion of the present day bitches are so full of " Mixer " or " Muddler " blood. As a show dog his wins under the best judges speak for themselves, and, in my opinion, taking him point by point, he has less faults than any Irish Terrier dog that has ever been seen. He is illustrated in here, together with Ch. Breda Muddler and Ch. Beeston Betty.

There are, of course, other dogs who have not earned a reputation on the show bench, and which have been successful sires in a moderate way, but space will not permit the subject to be carried further, beyond again impressing on breeders the desirability of ascertaining the true merits of a dog before they mate their bitches to him.

Notwithstanding those critics who are prone to swear by the dogs of by-gone days, and who declare that Irish Terriers of the present day have not improved as they should have done, the writer holds an entirely opposite opinion, and takes the liberty of suggesting that the lasting but erroneous impression which a youthful admiration often leaves, tends to warp their judgment.

Irish Terriers have made great progress in recent years, as is shown by the quality and evenness of the exhibits at the best Shows.

In the matter of coats, they have improved immensely and one rarely sees a really bad-coated one now.

The colour of eyes also has improved wonderfully, and yellow or gooseberry eyes are seldom seen on the Show bench. This was not the case years ago—and as regards carriage and size of ears, we do not want anything much better than they are. Dark shadings on the muzzle, which tend to give a sour expression, have also almost disappeared.

Legs and feet only remain to be commented on. Well, they are not equal to Fox Terriers', and they might be a little better or they might be worse—the bitches as a rule are worse than the dogs—but as a whole they are streets ahead of what they were years ago.

The late Mr. Geo. Krehl used to say that an Irish Terrier's foot should be fairly open and not too small, and others have said the same. They certainly must have good pads, and these must not be sacrificed for thin feet in order to give the appearance of "straight props" instead of symmetrical legs and feet; but, after all, there is nothing like a round tight foot with plenty of pad and the bone coming right down to it, without too much "waist" between the foot and the ankle. Compared with Wire Fox Terriers, which are so attractive in appearance, it must not be forgotten that the Irish Terrier is a larger dog and can never look quite so neat—nor is it wanted.

It can be truly said that Irish Terriers still hold their own in the estimation of the public whether as companions or when they are in the Show Ring. What should be striven for is the production of the most perfect dog that can be most honestly shown.

REGINALD EVERILL.

An excellent type of Irish Terrier, Champion Breda Muddler.

THE IRISH TERRIER

THE dare-devil Irish Terrier has most certainly made his home in our bosom. There is no breed of dog more genuinely loved by those who have sufficient experience and knowledge to make the comparison. Other dogs have a larger share of innate wisdom, others are most æsthetically beautiful, others more peaceable ; but our rufous friend has a way of winning into his owner's heart and making there an abiding place which is all the more secure because it is gained by sincere and undemonstrative devotion. Perhaps one likes him equally for his faults as for his merits. His very failings are due to his soldierly faithfulness and loyalty, to his too ardent vigilance in guarding the threshold, to his officious belligerence towards other canines who offend his sense of proprietorship in his master. , His particular stature may have some influence in his success as a chum. He is just tall enough to rest his chin upon one's knee and look up with all his soul into one's eyes. Whatever be the secret of his attraction 'tis certain that he has the Hibernian art of compelling affection and forgiveness, and that he makes one value him, not for the beauty of his ruddy raiment, the straightness of his fore-legs, the set of his eye and ear, the levelness of his back, or his ability to win prizes, but rather for his true and trusty heart, that exacts no return and seeks no recompense. He may be but an indifferent specimen of his kind, taken in as a stranger at the gates ; but when at length the inevitable time arrives, as it does all too soon in canine nature, one then discovers how surely one has been harbouring an angel unawares.

Statistics would probably show that in numbers the Fox-terrier justifies the reputation of being a more popular breed, and the Scottish Terrier is no doubt a formidable competitor for public esteem. It is safe, however, to say that the Irish Terrier shares with these the distinction of being one of the three most popular terriers in the British Isles.

This fact taken into consideration, it is interesting to reflect that thirty years ago the " Dare-Devil " was virtually unknown in England. Idstone, in his book on dogs, published in 1872 did not give a word of mention to the breed, and dog shows had been instituted sixteen years before a class was opened for the Irish Terrier. The dog existed, of course, in its native land. It may indeed be almost truthfully said to have existed " as long as that country has been an island."

About the year 1875, experts were in dispute over the Irish Terrier, and many averred that his rough coat and length of hair on forehead and muzzle were indubitable proof of Scotch blood. His very expression, they said, was Scotch. But the argument was quelled by more knowing disputants on the other side, who claimed that Ireland had never been without her terrier, and that she owed no manner of indebtedness to Scotland for a dog whose every hair was essentially Irish.

In the same year at a show held in Belfast a goodly number of the breed were brought together, notable among them being Mr. D. O'Connell's Slasher, a very good-looking wire-coated working terrier, who is said to have excelled as a field and water dog. Slasher was lint white in colour, and reputed to be descended from a pure white strain. Two other terriers of the time were Mr. Morton's Fly (the first Irish Terrier to gain a championship) and Mr. George Jamison's Sport.

The prominent Irish Terriers of the 'seventies varied considerably in type. Stinger, who won the first prize at Lisburn in 1875, was long-backed and short-legged, with a " dark blue grizzle coloured back, tan legs, and white turned-out feet." The dam of Mr. Burke's Killeney Boy was a rough black and tan, a combination of colours which was believed to

145

accompany the best class of coats. Brindles were not uncommon. Some were tall on the leg, some short; some were lanky and others cobby; many were very small. There were classes given at a Dublin show in 1874 for Irish Terriers under 9 lb. weight.

Jamison's Sport is an important dog historically, for various reasons. He was undoubtedly more akin to our present type than any other Irish Terrier of his time of which there is record. His dark ears were uncropped at a period when cropping was general; his weight approximated to our modern average. He was an all coloured red, and his legs were of a length that would not now be seriously objected to. But in his day he was not accepted as typical, and he was not particularly successful in the show ring. The distinguished terrier of his era was Burke's Killeney Boy, to whom, and to Mr. W. Graham's bitch Erin, with whom he was mated, nearly all the pedigrees of the best Irish Terriers of to-day date back. Erin was said to be superior in all respects to any of her breed previous to 1880. In her first litter by Killeney Boy were Play Boy, Pretty Lass, Poppy, Gerald, Pagan II., and Peggy, every one of whom became famous. More than one of these showed the black markings of their granddam, and their progeny for several generations were apt to throw back to the black-and-tan, grey, or brindle colouring. Play Boy and Poppy were the best of Erin's first litter. The dog's beautiful ears, which were left as Nature made them, were transmitted to his son Bogie Rattler, who was sire of Bachelor and Benedict, the latter the most successful stud dog of his time. Poppy had a rich red coat, and this colour recurred with fair regularity in her descendants. Red, which had not at first been greatly appreciated, came gradually to be the accepted colour of an Irish Terrier's jacket. Occasionally it tended towards flaxen; occasionally to a deep rich auburn; but the black and brindle were so rigidly bred out that by the year 1890, or thereabout, they very seldom recurred. Nowadays it is not often that any other colour than red is seen in a litter of Irish Terriers, although a white patch on the breast is frequent, as it is in all self-coloured breeds.

In addition to the early celebrities already named, Extreme Carelessness, Michael, Brickbat, Poppy II., Moya Doolan, Straight Tip, and Gaelic have taken their places in the records of the breed, while yet more recent Irish Terriers who have achieved fame have been Mrs. Butcher's Bawn Boy and Bawn Beauty, Mr. Wallace's Treasurer, Mr. S. Wilson's Bolton Woods Mixer, Dr. Smyth's Sarah Kidd, and Mr. C. J. Barnett's Breda Muddler.

Naturally in the case of a breed which has departed from its original type, discussions were frequent before a standard of perfection for the Irish Terrier was fixed. His size and weight, the length or shortness of his limbs, the carriage of his tail, the form of his skull and muzzle, the colour and texture of his coat were the subjects of controversy. It was considered at one juncture that he was being bred too big, and at another that he was being brought too much to resemble a red wirehair Fox-terrier. When once the black marking on his body had been eliminated no one seems to have desired that it should be restored. Red was acknowledged to be the one and only colour for an Irish Terrier. But some held that the correct red should be deep auburn, and others that wheaten colour was the tone to be aimed at. A medium shade between the two extremes is now generally preferred. As to size, it should be about midway between that of the Airedale and the Fox-terrier, represented by a weight of from 22 to 27 lb.

The two breeds just mentioned are, as a rule, superior to the Irish Terrier in front legs, and feet, but in the direction of these points great improvements have recently been observable. The heads of our Irish Terriers have also been brought nearer to a level of perfection, chiselled to the desired degree of leanness, with the determined expression so characteristic of the breed, and with the length, squareness, and strength of muzzle which formerly were so difficult to find. This squareness of head and jaw is an important point to be considered when choosing an Irish Terrier.

Opinions differ in regard to slight details of this terrier's conformation, but the official description, issued by the Irish Terrier Club, supplies a guide upon which the uncertain novice may implicitly depend :—

Head—Long ; skull flat, and rather narrow between ears, getting slightly narrower towards the eye ; free from wrinkles ; stop hardly visible except in profile. The jaw must be strong and muscular, and not too full in the cheek, and of a good punishing length. There should be a slight falling away below the eye, so as not to have a Greyhound appearance. Hair on face of same description as on body, but short (about a quarter of an inch long), in appearance almost smooth and straight ; a slight beard is the only longish hair (and it is only long in comparison with the rest) that is permissible, and this is characteristic. **Teeth**—Should be strong and level. **Lips**—Not so tight as a Bull-terrier's, but well-fitting, showing through the hair their black lining. **Nose**—Must be black. **Eyes**—A dark hazel colour, small, not prominent, and full of life, fire, and intelligence. **Ears**—Small and V-shaped, of moderate thickness, set well on the head, and dropping forward closely to the cheek. The ear must be free of fringe, and the hair thereon shorter and darker in colour than the body. **Neck**—Should be of a fair length, and gradually widening towards the shoulders, well carried, and free of throatiness. There is generally a slight sort of frill visible at each side of the neck, running nearly to the corner of the ear. **Shoulders and Chest**—Shoulders must be fine, long, and sloping well into the back ; the chest deep and muscular, but neither full nor wide. **Back and Loin**—Body moderately long; back should be strong and straight, with no appearance of slackness behind the shoulders ; the loin broad and powerful, and slightly arched ; ribs fairly sprung, rather deep than round, and well ribbed back. **Hind-quarters**—Should be strong and muscular, thighs powerful, hocks near ground, stifles moderately bent. **Stern**—Generally docked ; should be free of fringe or feather, but well covered with rough hair, set on pretty high, carried gaily, but not over the back or curled. **Feet and Legs**—Feet should be strong, tolerably round, and moderately small ; toes arched, and neither turned out nor in ; black toe nails most desirable. Legs moderately long, well set from the shoulders, perfectly straight, with plenty of bone and muscle ; the elbows working freely clear of the sides ; pasterns short and straight, hardly noticeable. Both fore and hind legs should be moved straight forward when travelling, the stifles not turned outwards, the legs free of feather, and covered, like the head, with as hard a texture of coat as body, but not so long. **Coat**—Hard and wiry, free of softness or silkiness, not so long as to hide the outlines of the body, particularly in the hind-quarters, straight and flat, no shagginess, and free of lock or curl. **Colour**—Should be " whole-coloured," the most preferable being bright red, red, wheaten, or yellow

red. White sometimes appears on chest and feet; it is more ob
jectionable on the latter than on the chest, as a speck of white on chest
is frequently to be seen in all self-coloured breeds. **Size and Symmetry**
—The most desirable weight in show condition is, for a dog 24 lb., and
for a bitch 22 lb. The dog must present an active, lively, lithe, and
wiry appearance ; lots of substance, at the same time free of clumsiness,
as speed and endurance, as well as power, are very essential. They
must be neither cloddy or cobby, but should be framed on the lines of
speed, showing a graceful racing outline. **Temperament**—Dogs that
are very game are usually surly or snappish. The Irish Terrier as
a breed is an exception, being remarkably good-tempered, notably
so with mankind, it being admitted, however, that he is perhaps a little
too ready to resent interference on the part of other dogs. There is a
heedless, reckless pluck about the Irish Terrier which is characteristic,
and, coupled with the headlong dash, blind to all consequences, with
which he rushes at his adversary, has earned for the breed the proud
epithet of " The Dare-Devils." When " off-duty " they are characterised by a quiet, caress-inviting appearance, and when one sees
them endearingly, timidly pushing their heads into their masters' hands,
it is difficult to realise that on occasions, at the " set on," they can
prove they have the courage of a lion, and will fight unto the last
breath in their bodies. They develop an extraordinary devotion to
and have been known to track their masters almost incredible
distances.

It is difficult to refer to particular Irish Terriers of to-day
without making invidious distinctions. There are so many
excellent examples of the breed that a list even of those who
have gained championship honours would be formidable.
But one would hardly hesitate to head the list with the name
of Paymaster, a dog of rare and almost superlative quality
and true Irish Terrier character. Paymaster is the property
of Miss Lilian Paull, of Weston-super-Mare, who bred him
from her beautiful bitch Erasmic from Breda Muddler, the sire
of many of the best. Side by side with Paymaster, Mr. F.
Clifton's Mile End Barrister might be placed. It would need
a council of perfection, indeed, to decide which is the better
dog of the two. Very high in the list, also, would come Mr.
Henry Ridley's Redeemer and Mr. Breakell's Killarney Sport.
And among bitches one would name certainly Mr. Gregg's
Belfast Erin, Mr. Clifton's Charwoman, Mr. Everill's Erminie,
and Mr. J. S. McComb's Beeston Betty. These are but half
a dozen, but they represent the highest level of excellence

that has yet been achieved by scientific breeding in Irish Terrier type.

Breeding up to the standard of excellence necessary in competition in dog shows has doubtless been the agent which has brought the Irish Terrier to its present condition of perfection, and it is the means by which the general dog owning public is most surely educated to a practical knowledge of what is a desirable and what an undesirable dog to possess. But, after all, success in the show ring is not the one and only thing to be aimed at, and the Irish Terrier is not to be regarded merely as the possible winner of prizes. He is above all things a dog for man's companionship, and in this capacity he takes a favoured place. He has the great advantage of being equally suitable for town and country life. In the home he requires no pampering ; he has a good, hardy constitution, and when once he has got over the ills incidental to puppyhood—worms and distemper—he needs only to be judiciously fed, kept reasonably clean, and to have his fill of active exercise. If he is taught to be obedient and of gentlemanly habit, there is no better house dog. He is naturally intelligent and easily trained. Although he is always ready to take his own part, he is not quarrelsome, but remarkably good-tempered and a safe associate of children. Perhaps with his boisterous spirits he is prone sometimes to be over-zealous in the pursuit of trespassing tabbies and in assailing the ankles of intruding butcher boys and officious postmen. These characteristics come from his sense of duty, which is strongly developed, and careful training will make him discriminative in his assaults.

Very justly is he classed among the sporting dogs. He is a born sportsman, and of his pluck it were superfluous to speak. Fear is unknown to him. In this characteristic as in all others, he is truly a son of Erin.

THE IRISH TERRIER

A fighter who enters the list with a rush, hurling himself at his foe, without any thought as to results. Hot-tempered dog as far as other dogs are concerned, but one of the kindest-hearted. A favourite house dog.

Weight, about 26 lb. (bitches 24 lb), a wiry, alive, quick, well-built active Terrier. The coat hard and wiry, not soft, curly, or shaggy. Body moderately long, chest narrow, back straight and ribs fairly well sprung. Colours, various shades from a light to a brown red. Colour even. Nose black, eyes hazel, and small ears, V-shaped, no fringe, covered with short silky hair, darker than body. Occasionally a white patch on chest, not wanted but allowed ; white feet also occur. Too much white is a fault.

As well as a show dog, few are better for vermin, keener on foxes, and better ' pals.' First known in England about 1875. The Irish Terrier Club was formed four years later.

A TYPICAL IRISH TERRIER, CHAMPION BOLDON
BOY, owned by Mr. Will Slater, Stratford
House, East Boldon, Co. Durham.

THE IRISH TERRIER

It was in 1872 that the Irish Terrier (in their early days popularly known as *The Dare Devil or Wild Irishman*) was first introduced to the public, who were then informed that a breed of excellent Terriers peculiar to Ireland were to be found there, distinct from all other Terriers. They had **pedigrees** that would take them back **many hundreds of years.** So much had been said that the Dublin Show Committee, the following year, arranged a class for the claimed old-established breed. The judge, not knowing which was the right breed, no two exhibits being much alike, happened to remember all at once a letter of a recent correspondent on Irish Terriers, signed *Celt*, and discovering such a dog gave first prize to it. This was *Celt's* dog. On reporting the class, the *Live Stock Journal* remarked that the Terriers exhibited of so many kinds had no better reason to be called Irish than that they had been born on the Island ! To understand the coming of the breed, we must know that in 1874 the Dublin Show Committee again offered prizes for Irish Terriers, but this time for dogs under 9 pounds *in weight*, and in 1875 a pure-bred Irish Terrier, a white dog, won a first prize ! In 1876 again an attempt was made to establish the variety. Two classes were arranged for Dublin Show, one for dogs above 16 pounds

¹ See Plate 8, No. 22.　　² See Plate 28, No. 13.

and one for those below that weight. The judge chosen was reputed to be a leading breeder of Irish Terriers, who had kept the *Wild Irishmen* for twenty or thirty years. It was anticipated, therefore, that his arrangement of the exhibits would end the controversy as to the proper type, a matter which had never been satisfactorily settled. The Committee, fearing that confusion and ridicule would be caused should the class be subjected to the reappearance of mongrels, such as had been previously exhibited, stipulated that no entries could be accepted unless accompanied by a pedigree. It was, therefore, expected that this show would be the first representative gathering of the pure old breed of Irish Terrier, and it was awaited with considerable interest. On the morning of the show Mr. Merry, the judge, arrived. Thirty-four dogs awaited him. The stipulation as to pedigree had apparently not had the desired effect. The exhibits varied in size, in shape, and in colour. The dogs were of many kinds. Some weighed well over 35 pounds and others 16 pounds and less. It was not an easy class to judge. Whilst the judge was examining the exhibits he was disturbed by a very angry young man, who, having watched him for a time, came down from the gallery and rudely accosted him, accusing him of *not knowing how to judge.* He, however, continued judging, and gave first prize to a pepper-coloured dog, and also to this exhibit the cup for the *best Irish Terrier in the show.* The judging over, the awards were subjected to the most violent abuse. The winner of the cup, evidently a mongrel, was blind, and its eyes were a most unpleasant sight, and it was therefore disqualified. In the other class the second prize was awarded to a dog of a deep yellow colour, but somebody examining the exhibit came to the conclusion that the hair on the top of its head had been treated with dye, and the Committee, after examination, disqualified it. The owner of the dog protested, and refused to be stilled, and a little later, much to the relief of the Committee, was seen hurrying out of the show taking his dog with him ! But an hour or so later he had returned. He took the dog to the Committee-room and demanded *fair play* ! He had been wrongly accused of fraud. Here was the dog ! He had brought it to them to see. The colour of the hair on the head was the dog's proper colour, *let them show him* any dyed hair ! They stood round half angry, half amused. A strange dog it now appeared to be ! The coat ended just above its cheeks. The top of its head had **been recently shaved.** The owner repeated his innocence. Show me the dyed hair, he demanded !

It needs no statement of mine to suggest the difficulty the pedigrees must have caused those who entered the miscellaneous collection.[1] I wish that it were possible to give an entire list. We must be satisfied with one.

" **Pedigree :** Breeder, one of the famous Limerick Night Watch. Pedigree too long to give, but *inquisitive* people *can* inquire at the Watch House here, and *most likely* they will be told."

It was the same year, and partly due to what had happened at this show, that Dr. Carey started his kennel of Irish Terriers. He had won first prize at the show with a little bitch that he had, so he stated, picked up at a nominal price in the streets of Dublin. He admitted later that it was a very poor specimen of the breed, but, all the same, winning an honour made him feel inclined to see if he could not bring out a first-class dog. Later he purchased a dog named Ch. *Sport*[2] from Mr. Jameson, of Belfast,

[1] Mr. Merry later wrote to the Press that the dogs he had given prizes to, described by the Press as *mongrels*, were indeed dogs of long, pure breeding, " carefully bred for over a century."

[2] This Terrier, I see from an illustration, was a strongly built, good type of Irish Terrier, as an Irish Terrier appears to-day before it is trimmed.

who apparently had the best type of Terrier, for he had won by 1876 fifty-four prizes. Dr. Carey was instrumental in the forming of the Irish Terrier Club in 1879, giving the first *official* standard of the breed. The first standard had, however, been drawn up four years previously by someone who named himself *Shamrock*. Mr. Walsh published these points in his book. Mr. Walsh was careful ; he had the points signed by twenty-five leading breeders and exhibitors, with their qualifications, under the heading, " If an exhibitor, state number of prizes taken." These twenty-five signatures relieved him of much responsibility.[1] Into the story of the Irish Terrier entered *Killeney Boy*,[2] affectionately known as the *Old Tyke*. He was bred by Mr. Burke, of Queen Street, Dublin. He came into the hands of a Mr. Flanagham, but how he obtained the *Old Tyke* I do not know. Mr. Flanagham, when he left his house, having sold it to a Mr. Donnegan, left the dog behind him. Mr. Donnegan, not requiring a dog, gave the dog to Mr. Howard Waterhouse. *Killeney Boy's* mother was a rough black-and-tan. He was on the small side, a trifle light in bone, whilst his coat was too open, and he had the best of hocks. But he had the neatest of heads, and the wisest of faces— a great depth around his heart, and he was " as game as you make them," and a cheery little fellow, too ! This dog was the sire of *Erin's* puppies. Time passed, and from " *Erin's* puppies " many of the best dogs in Irish history were descended. The enthusiasm of the Irish Terrier breeders as time went on increased. Into the breed had come many well-known English dog-breeders, including Mr. Krehl. Dalziel watched the enthusiastic claims of the *Irish Terrier men* with no little amusement. Indeed, he never ceased to attack them ! His attacks centred on Mr. Krehl. In 1881 Dalziel's little war against the Irish Terrier and Krehl came to a head. A letter appeared in the *Stock-keeper*, signed *Sirius*, in which he wrote :—

" Walking leisurely along Bond Street on Sunday afternoon, I spotted a gentleman pretty well known as an Irish Terrier fancier—I won't mention *his* name--accompanied by three of his paddy pets. Immediately in my front were two London costers in Sunday best. Says one to the other : ' See, Bill, There's an Ikey rat-catcher for you ! ' To which Bill replied, admiringly : ' Aye, rorty bloke, ain't 'e ? Dessay 'e 's rat-ketcher to the Queen.' "

There was no need to inquire who the attack was meant for, because, apart from all else, Mr. Krehl had visited Queen Victoria's kennels. He had presented Her Majesty with one or two Irish Terriers. Krehl was not over pleased, to judge from the tone of his reply. He writes in his letter that he had purchased a slang dictionary, the price of which he hoped the *Stock-keeper* would refund him.

In 1889 Vero Shaw's *Book of the Dog* appeared. In it Mr. Krehl wrote the section dealing with the Irish Terrier. It is certainly an astonishing section. He divided his subject into eight headings. The first was *Pluck*, then came *Rabbiting*, then *Stamina*, followed by one marked *Badger, Foxes, Otters, Water Rats*, etc. Under each of these heading he wrote a paragraph in which he stated that the Irish Terrier was **peculiarly suited** to the work, or was more than commonly capable at it. It was the **best** dog for pluck, the **most** astute rabbiter, it had the **most outstanding** stamina, it faced badgers like no other dog dare face them ; it was the dog most feared by foxes, and when it came to *rats* Mr. Krehl's enthusiasm had reached a climax ! The Irish Terrier would kill rats at an absurdly youthful age. An Irish Terrier had no need to shake them ! " They were not big enough for that " (!) We must regretfully pass by many years of Irish Terrier history, of *Playboy*

---

[1] This list of qualifications is an amusing one. An example : " Thomas Erwin Breeder and exhibitor, 1 prize."   [2] Often given as Killiney Boy.

and *Garryowen*, of the coming of *Brickbat* and *Breda Mixer*, and of *Cahron*, his son, which weighed 23 pounds, the winner of seventeen prizes, and which was, in the year 1895, considered the most typical Irish Terrier ever seen.

There is a story of two Englishmen on a visit to Dublin who all at once noticed from the carriage in which they were driving a man and a dog going along the street. One glance sufficed to show the dog to be a remarkable specimen of Irish Terrier. They impressed upon the driver the importance to follow, until the man with the dog went into a public house. They found him near the bar. They plied him with many drinks, and got into conversation. The dog was on the show bench in England ; the bench covered with red cards ! At last they led the man to mention what *he thought* the value of the dog. " *Eight pounds*," the man had said ! They might have gasped. The finest Irish Terrier they had seen—eight pounds ! They could scarcely believe—eight pounds ! Hurriedly they held out the money to him. But he hesitated, then explained. Before he could settle the matter he would have to ask his master !

A victory merely deferred ! They asked who his master was ; eight pounds would be useful to him ! " Mr. Weiner ? Good gracious, this is *Brickbat*," they cried together.[1] " Yes—that's the name," said the man. *Brickbat* died in 1895. He had won the sixty-guinea cup a dozen times.

Another noted dog was *Bolton Woods Mixer*,[2] bought for £10. He earned his master £300 a year in stud fees and prizes, and won 2,000 prizes and 100 championships ! He stood at stud at £3 3s., and it is said that his owner, Mr. Sam Wilson, of Bradford, refused £700 for him. He was known as *Sam Wilson's Bread Winner*. He lived to a good age. He was twelve years old when he died.

In more recent years we find *Botanic Demon*, Mr. J. J. Holgate's dog, the most important winning *Irish Terrier*, and Miss L. A. Paull's *Musbury Mavourneen*. Mrs. O. W. Porritt, a most important owner of " Wild Irishmen," exhibited the famous *Barlae Brickbat* and *Musbury Demon*. Later we find Mr. A. B. Montgomery exhibiting his important dog *Celtic Judy* and *Celtic Pal*, and *Celtic Poplin* and *Celtic Sweetheart*. Mr. N. Galloway showed *Cringle Begorra*, and Mr. W. S. Green his *Galloper*, and Mr. E. Perfect his *Boy*.

THE IRISH TERRIER.

Head : Long ; skull flat, and rather narrow between ears, getting slightly narrower towards the eye ; **free from wrinkles ; stop** hardly visible except in profile. The jaw must be strong and muscular, but not too full in the cheek, and of a good punishing length. There is a slight falling away below the eye, so as not to have a Greyhound appearance. **Hair on face** of same description as on body, but short (about a quarter of an inch long), in appearance almost smooth and straight ; a slight **beard** is permissible, the only longish hair (and it is only long in comparison with the rest). **Teeth :** Strong and level. **Lips :** Not so tight as a Bull Terrier's, but well fitting, showing through the hair their black lining. **Nose :** Black. **Eyes :** A dark hazel colour, small, not prominent, but full of life, fire, and intelligence. **Ears :** Small and V-shaped, of moderate thickness, set well on the head, and dropping forward closely to the cheek. The ear free of fringe, and the hair thereon shorter and darker in colour than the body. **Neck :** A fair length, gradually widening towards the shoulders, well carried, and free of throatiness. There is generally a slight sort of frill visible at each side of the neck, running nearly to the corner of the ear. **Shoulders :** Fine, long and sloping well into the back ; the **chest** deep and muscular, but neither full nor wide. **Body :** moderately long ; **back** strong and straight, with no appearance of slackness behind the shoulders ; the **loin** broad and powerful and slightly arched ; **ribs** fairly sprung, rather deep than round, and well ribbed back. **Hindquarters :** Strong and muscular, the thighs powerful, hocks near the ground, stifles moderately bent. **Stern :** Generally docked ; free of fringe or feather, but well covered with rough hair, set on pretty high, carried gaily, but not over the back or curled. **Feet :** Neither turned out nor in, strong, tolerably round, and toes moderately small, arched. Black toe-nails most desirable. **Legs** moderately long, well set from the shoulders, perfectly straight, with plenty of bone and muscle ; the elbows working freely clear of the sides ; pasterns short and straight, hardly noticeable. Both **fore** and **hind legs** move straight forward when travelling, the stifles not turned outwards, the legs free of feather and covered, like the head, with as hard a texture

157

of coat as body, but not so long. **Coat :** Hard and wiry, free of softness or silkiness, not so long as to hide the outlines of the body, particularly in the hindquarters, straight and flat, no shagginess, locks or curls. Whole **coloured.** The most preferable bright red, red-wheaten, or yellow-red. White sometimes appears on chest and feet ; it is more objectionable on the feet than on the chest. A speck of white on chest is frequently to be seen on all self-coloured breeds. The most desirable **weight** in Show condition is 27 lb. for a dog, and 25 lb. for a bitch. The dog must present an active, lively, lithe and wiry appearance ; **substance** without **clumsiness,** as speed and endurance, as well as power, are very essential. Dogs must be neither " cloddy nor cobby."

POINTS.

Head, ears and expression	20
Legs and feet	15
Neck	5
Shoulders and chest	10
Back and loin	5
Hindquarters and stern	10
Coat	15
Colour	10
Size and symmetry	10
Total	100

DEDUCTIONS.

White nails, toes and feet,	minus	10
Much white on chest	,,	10
Dark shadings on face	,,	5
Mouth undershot or cankered	,,	10
Coat shaggy, curly or soft	,,	10
Uneven in colour	,,	5

THE IRISH TERRIER

Origin and History.—One has to admit regretfully that Irish Terriers, for the moment, are in a bad way, a rapid decline having occurred within the last few years. If you ask breeders what it is that has brought about this unfortunate state of affairs, you will probably get answers that are unprintable, not because of the bad language used, but out of respect to the law of libel. The conclusion one is compelled to reach is that the dogs are not so much to blame as internal dissensions among those who are supposed to be supporters of the breed. There are differences about size and other matters that seem to make people pick and choose their judges and not to support shows vigorously merely for the good of the dog. It is a thousand pities, because the Irish Terrier at one time was a force in the show world and was much liked by the general public. As a matter of fact, he is still a favourite housedog, and there are enough in the country to give support to classes at shows if exhibitors would only pull together instead of standing aloof.

It may be said that the Irish Terrier is a compromise between the Fox Terrier and Airedale, and that he is built on more racy lines than either. All sorts of theories have been advanced concerning the origin of these terriers. Some writers have suggested that they are a compound between several other terriers with a dash of bulldog in them, while others contend that they are of the same type as the Irish Wolfhound but smaller. I should think the most probable explanation is that for many centuries a sporting country like Ireland had a race of terriers which were capable of doing any sort of work that came along, and that from selected specimens of these the red-coated Irish Terrier has been evolved in one direction and the Kerry Blue in another. The point is really not worth pursuing to any extent, the most interesting part of his history being his development during the show period.

A good deal of light was thrown upon this subject in some articles contributed to *Our Dogs* in 1926 by Mr. James Brabazon of Lisburn, County Antrim. Although I thought I knew something about Irish Terriers, I was surprised to read there that when they were first given a distinct classification at Dublin in 1873 classes were divided by weight, one being for dogs under 9 lb. and the other for dogs of 9 lb. and over. Two years later at Cork the minimum weight was raised to 12 lb., and at Dublin in 1876 it was advanced to 16 lb. In the early years of the Irish Terrier Club, founded in 1879, the weight most favoured, I believe, was near to, but under, 22 lb. Later on that was fixed as the maximum weight for bitches, that for dogs being raised to 24 lb., and so it remained until 1925, when the maximum for dogs was agreed at 27 lb. and for bitches at 25 lb. The colour also was at one time subject to a good deal of variation, but in later times bright red has had the preference, although red-wheaten or yellow-red are also recognisable. I have seen it said that a golden-red is a good colour because it cannot well be tampered with by unscrupulous exhibitors, but that is scarcely correct, as a famous case once came before the Kennel Club in which the colour of a prominent winner had been improved by the application of brown boot polish.

One of the foremost breeders told me that most of the earlier show dogs had a tendency to grow light-coloured, linty coats that came much too long. Dogs of this sort had usually the longest and leanest heads, and those with coats of the best texture and colour had, generally speaking, the worst heads. This trouble about the soft coats was surmounted long ago, though, of course, we get them occasionally.

From 1890 onwards large classes of the red terriers were common at all shows, and good prices were realised by the best, though they have never equalled those paid for Fox Terriers, Airedales and Sealyhams. Even since the War the demand was so satisfactory at first that *Brentmoor Bewitched* is said to have bred £1,000 worth of puppies for Mr. Pritchard. Then a sort of dry rot set in. The trouble is not beyond remedy, however, and I hope that before long justice will be done to a very fine dog. As it happens, the public, knowing nothing about differences in the show world, still chooses to think that these dogs are desirable companions and we see plenty of them in the streets. Contrary to the usual opinion, Hazlitt once wrote that a nickname is the hardest stone that the devil can throw at a man. Surely he was wrong, for nearly every man who rejoices in a nickname has some endearing quality or force of character. The sobriquet of " daredevil " commonly bestowed upon the Irish Terrier must be taken in a complimentary sense, and all who have had anything to do with him will agree that it is deserved.

A paragraph in the standard of the Irish Terrier Club may seem a little eulogistic, but it is certainly applicable :

161

" Dogs that are very game are usually surly or snappish. The Irish Terrier as a breed is an exception, being remarkably good-tempered, notably so with mankind, it being admitted, however, that he is perhaps a little too ready to resent interference on the part of other dogs. There is a heedless, reckless pluck about the Irish Terrier which is characteristic, and, coupled with the headlong dash, blind to all consequences, with which he rushes at his adversary, has earned for the breed the proud epithet of ' the daredevils.' When off duty they are characterised by a quiet, caress-inviting appearance, and when one sees them endearingly, timidly pushing their heads into their masters' hands, it is difficult to realise that on occasions, at the set on, they can prove they have the courage of a lion and will fight unto the last breath in their bodies. They develop an extraordinary devotion to, and have been known to track their masters incredible distances."

Standard Description.—In considering the ideal Irish Terrier, we must remember that he is somewhat racy of build, presenting an active, lively, lithe and wiry appearance. He wants to have plenty of substance and yet be free from clumsiness so that he may have speed and endurance as well as power. *Head.*—The head is long, the skull flat and rather narrow between the ears, decreasing slightly in breadth towards the eye. There is scarcely any stop, and the jaw must be strong and muscular, of a good punishing length. The eyes are dark hazel, small, not prominent, and full of fire and intelligence. Ears small and V-shaped, of moderate thickness, dropping forward closely to the cheek. There should be no fringe, and the hair on the leather is shorter and darker in colour than that of the body. The neck must be of fair length, gradually widening towards the shoulders, carried well up and free from throatiness. Shoulders should be long and sloping ; the chest deep and muscular, but neither full nor wide. The body must be moderately long, and the back strong and straight. Loins must be broad and powerful and slightly arched. Ribs fairly sprung, rather deep than round, and carried well back. *Legs.*—The front legs are not so dead true as those of a Fox Terrier, but for all that, short and straight pasterns are required. The legs are of moderate length and have plenty of bone and muscle. They are free from feather and covered, like the head, with as hard a texture of coat as that on the body, but not so long. *Feet.*—The feet should be strong, tolerably round and moderately small. Hindquarters must be strong and muscular. Hocks near the ground. The docked stern should be free of fringe or feather, but well covered with rough hair ; it should be set on pretty high, carried gaily but not over the back or curled. *Coat.*— The coat is hard, wiry and not so long as to hide the outlines of the body, particularly on the hindquarters. It must be straight and flat without shagginess and free from curl. *Colour.*—The dogs are whole-coloured. The most preferable is a bright red, a red-wheaten or a yellow-red. A speck of white on the chest is frequently seen. White is more objectionable on the feet than on the chest.

THE IRISH TERRIER

THE Irish Terrier is without doubt a remarkable animal, and possesses many sterling qualities. We often hear him referred to as the " Daredevil Irish Red," due no doubt to his indomitable courage. He is a dog that possesses many true qualities. His chief fault, if it can be called a fault, is his excitable disposition, and, to use the Irish phrase, he

IRISH TERRIER

soon gets his paddy up. Some breeds are born fighters, some achieve fights, and some have fights thrust upon them; but with a true Irish Terrier, if trouble is thrust upon him, he will never put off till tomorrow that which he can do today.

Like most terriers, this dog was, and is still, used in Ireland for rabbiting, fox-bolting, and ratting, for all of which he is suitable. His Hibernian qualities have won him many friends; his ardent vigilance, coupled with his sincere and undemonstrative devotion, makes him a real chum, and his convenient size should be a reason for greater popularity.

Irish Terrier breeders claim for the breed long and pure descent, although no direct proof of this can be given; and less than thirty years ago, amongst Irishmen themselves, opposite opinions were publicly expressed as to what an Irish Terrier was like, and the utmost difficulty was experienced in getting those who were interested in the breed to band themselves together and agree upon a universal standard being adopted, as at that time every Irishman thought he possessed the best specimen possible, with the result that there was some criticism of the awards made at shows where the breed was scheduled, and those who judged had anything but a happy experience at the finish of their duties. As soon as an agreed standard was adopted the breed began to be distributed universally; classes were scheduled for them at more shows, and the " Dare-devil Irish Red " took his position amongst the aristocrats of the canine world.

The Irish Terrier has the courage of a lion, and will fight to the last breath in his body. As a guard and companion he is wonderful. His small, dark, hazel-coloured eyes are full of fire, life, and intelligence; and his moderately long back (as level as a table-top), strong and muscular hind-quarters, and bearded face, all add to his beauty and charm. He is a very active animal, and weighs approximately 22 to 24 pounds.

THE EARLY IRISH TERRIERS

The Irish Terrier also has been altered by the Fancier since its most important days. On the top we see Mr. E. A. Wiener's Ch. "Brickbat" (the finest Irish Terrier ever seen—so they said at the time), its ears cropped, and below we have Mr. Pim's noted dog, Ch. "Play Boy," another of the greatest dogs of its day

THE IRISH TERRIER   CH. STRONGHEART SENSATION

It is over sixty years ago since the " Wild Irishman," as he was then known, was first exhibited, although the breed had been known in Ireland for hundreds of years.

It is claimed that the Little Irishman is a pure-bred dog, although in certain circles there appears to be an idea that there is a certain amount of fox terrier in the dog. Of course, the colours are entirely different, but the sizes are approximately the same. This dog is rather pugnacious but plucky in the extreme. Like most other terriers, he is tireless, very affectionate, but the very " divil " when roused.

167

THE IRISH TERRIER

HEAD : Long but proportionate : skull flat and rather narrow between the ears, getting slightly narrower towards the eye ; free from wrinkle ; stop hardly visible except in profile. The foreface should not " dish " or fall away quickly, between and below the eyes, where it should be well made up, being relieved from " wedginess " by delicate chiselling. Both upper and lower jaws must be strong and muscular and of a good punishing length, but an exaggerated foreface which is out of proportion to the skull not only spoils the balance of the head, but gives a dog a " foreign " appearance. Furthermore, an exaggerated length of head is usually attached to an oversized or long-backed specimen, both of which are bad faults. If, however, the foreface is palpably shorter than the skull (or in other words than from the stop to the occiput), it amounts to a fault, the head looking weak and unfinished. An excessive muscular development of the cheeks, or bony development of the temples— usually described as " cheeky " or " thick in head "—is unsightly and wrong. What are termed " alligator heads " also—that is, where the skull has two bony lumps and probably two indentations above the eyes—are an abomination and altogether opposed to the correct head. The hair on the upper and lower jaws should be crisp and only sufficiently long to impart an appearance of additional strength to the foreface. A beard like a " goat " is suggestive of there being silky and bad hair running through the coat generally. TEETH : Should be strong, even, free from canker, and the top teeth slightly overlapping the lower. LIPS : Should be well fitting and, externally, almost black in colour. NOSE : Must be black. EYES : Should be dark in colour, moderately small not prominent, and full of life, fire and intelligence. A yellow or light eye is most objectionable. EARS : Small and V-shaped, of moderate thickness, set well on the head, and dropping forward close to the cheek. The top line of the folded ear should be well above the level of the skull. An ear hanging dead by the side of the head, like a hound's, is not characteristic of the Terrier, while an ear which is semi-erect is still more undesirable. The hair on the ear should be short, and is usually darker in colour than that on the body. NECK : Should be of a fair length and gradually widening towards the shoulders, well carried, and free of throatiness.

SHOULDERS and CHEST : Shoulders must be fine, long, and sloping well into the back ; the chest deep and muscular, but neither full nor wide. BACK and LOINS : Body should be symmetrical—neither too long nor too short ; back should be strong and straight, with no appearance of slackness behind the shoulders ; the loins muscular and very slightly arched ; ribs fairly sprung, rather deep than round, and well ribbed back. A bitch may be slightly longer in couplings than a dog. HINDQUARTERS : Should be strong and muscular, the thighs powerful, hocks near the ground, stifles moderately bent. STERN : Should be set on rather high but not curled. It should be of good strength and substance and fair length— a three-quarters dock is about right, well covered with hard, rough hair and free from fringe or feather.

FEET and LEGS : Feet should be strong, tolerably round, moderately small ; toes arched and neither turned out nor in, with black toe-nails. Pads must be absolutely sound and free from cracks or horny excrescences. The two latter usually run together and become more pronounced in hot and dry weather. In winter and damp weather the pads may temporarily improve, but the trouble will inevitably reappear sooner or later, resulting in unsoundness, and so far no permanent cure has been discovered ; but, even if there is a temporary cure, the disease is still there and will be handed down in breeding, and the only way to eradicate it entirely is to at all cost avoid breeding from dogs or bitches which show any evidence of the disease. Legs moderately long, well set from the shoulders, perfectly straight, with plenty of bone and muscle ; the elbows working freely clear of the sides ; pasterns short and straight, hardly noticeable. Both fore and hind-legs should be moved straight forward when travelling, the stifles not turned outwards. " Cow-hocks " —that is, where the hocks are turned in and the stifles and feet turned out, are a very serious detriment. The hair on the legs should be dense and crisp.

COAT : Should be dense and wiry in texture, having a broken appearance, but still lying fairly flat, the hairs growing so closely and strongly together that when parted with the fingers the skin cannot be seen ; free of softness or silkiness and not so long as to hide the outline of the body, particularly the hindquarters. At the base of these stiff hairs is a growth of finer and softer hair, usually a little darker in colour, termed the undercoat. Single coats or those without an undercoat are undesirable, and a wavy or curly coat is very objectionable. The coat on the sides is never quite so hard as that on the back and quarters, but there should be plenty of it. COLOUR : Should be " whole coloured," the most preferable being bright red, golden red, or red wheaten. A small patch of white on the chest is permissible, as this is frequently to be seen in all whole-coloured breeds.

SIZE and SYMMETRY : The most desirable weight in show condition is, for a dog 27 lb., and for a bitch 25 lb., and the height at shoulder approximately 18 inches. The dog must present an active, lively, lithe and wiry appearance, lots of substance, at the same time free of clumsiness, as speed and endurance as well as power are very essential. They must be neither " cloddy nor cobby," but should be framed on the " lines of speed," showing a graceful " racing outline." Notwithstanding the " desirable " weights mentioned above, which are given as a guide, it is mainly a question of general appearance, and if a dog is oversized or undersized it is easily discernible in the show ring, whatever his or her weight may be. The actual weight therefore, regardless of other considerations, must not become an obsession, otherwise the wrong type of dog may be brought to the front. For instance, a comparatively small, heavily-made, cloddy dog—which is not what is wanted—may easily be the standard weight or over it, whereas another which is long in leg, with not the necessary substance and built somewhat on the lines of a whippet—also not what is wanted—may be the exact weight or under it, which proves that, while the standard weights must be borne well in mind, it is not the " last word " in judging, the main thing being to select as far as possible those of the generally accepted moderate size, possessing the other necessary characteristics.

TEMPERAMENT.—The Irish Terrier, while being game and capable of holding his own with other dogs, is remarkably loyal, good tempered, and affectionate with mankind.

STANDARD OF POINTS

Head, Ears and Expression	..	..	..	..	..	20
Legs and Feet	..	..	..	..	..	15
Neck	..	..	..	..	..	5
Shoulders and Chest ..	..	..	..	..	..	10
Back and Loin	..	..	..	..	..	5
Hindquarters and Stern	..	..	..	..	..	10
Coat	..	..	..	..	..	15
Colour	..	..	..	..	..	10
Size and Symmetry ..	..	..	..	..	..	10
						100

Lightning Source UK Ltd.
Milton Keynes UK
UKOW05f1309220714

235548UK00001B/64/P